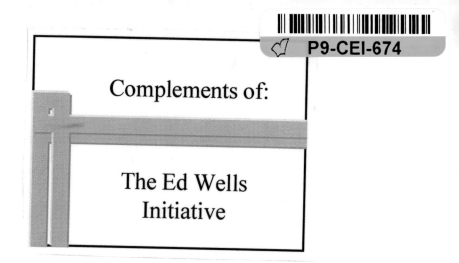

Complements of:

The Ed Wells
Initiative

Boeing's Ed Wells

BOEING'S
Ed Wells

Mary Wells Geer

Foreword by T. A. Wilson

UNIVERSITY OF WASHINGTON PRESS

Seattle and London

Library of Congress Cataloging-in-Publication Data

Geer, Mary Wells.
  Boeing's Ed Wells / Mary Wells Geer.
     p.   cm.
  Includes bibliographical references and index.
  ISBN 0-295-97204-1 (alk. paper)
  1. Wells, Edward Curtis, 1910–   . 2. Aerospace engineers—United
States—Biography.   3. Boeing Company—Officials and employees.
I. Title.
TL540.W399G44   1992
629.1′092—dc20
[B]   92-29582
                                                                                                   CIP

The paper used in this publication meets the minimum requirements of
American National Standard for Information Sciences—Permanence of Paper
for Printed Library Materials, ANSI Z39.48-1984.

Frontispiece: Edward C. Wells (photograph by Karsh)

Contents

Foreword

Ed Wells has made as much—if not more—of a contribution to the relative success of The Boeing Company as any other individual. He was a spectacular engineer, not only from the standpoint of intricate detail design, which he continued throughout his career, but also as a great systems integrator, whether the project was a commercial airplane, a military weapon system, or a space project. He was highly regarded by those in the aerospace industry, the ones who buy aerospace products, and the people in the institutions who supply us our engineers.

At Boeing, this unusual man affected every facet of the business whether or not it was under his direct line of control. All Boeing people had great respect for Ed, and the engineers adored him. This wonderful feeling of Boeing engineers stemmed from the kind of human being he was, as well as from recognition of his engineering talents. The latter has been reasonably well documented, but the human side not so well understood. Mary Wells Geer's book goes a long way toward giving its readers insight on how Ed became the kind of person he was.

T. A. Wilson

Preface

On January 12, 1950, Thomas Collison, creator of splendid books on Boeing planes, wrote to Ed Wells, saying, "We're still strongly of the opinion that someday you should write a think-piece anent 'Of Arms and Men.' And to this end, we hope you are keeping a diary."

Wells replied, "I regret to report that in spite of your suggestion, I have not yet started to keep a diary. Perhaps it is because there is as much to forget as there is to remember. Or, perhaps it is only because I am not industrious enough to do the work required in keeping a diary. Next time I am in Washington, D.C., however, I would like to talk to you about the subject, for I know you would not have made the suggestion unless you had a reason for it."

Following Ed's death in 1986, four large boxes were delivered into my keeping. These contained the record of almost seventy years of his life: pictures drawn when he was a child of five; letters back as far as high school; photos of his model planes and model railroads; oil paintings and watercolors; portraits; designs of every Boeing plane; official memoranda and calculations; patents; telegrams; newspaper clippings and magazine articles; notices of awards and biographical data; and speeches he had given.

I was overwhelmed with the richness of history represented by this hoard. I then realized that this was Ed Wells' diary carefully saved through the years—a diary only awaiting an editing. This I have attempted to do, letting Ed Wells, the aviation genius and gentle man, as often as possible, record his story in his own words and in the words others used to describe him.

Mary Wells Geer

1

Early Years

In July 1985, more than two thousand pilots and crewmen of the Flying Fortress bombers, together with their families and television crews for two documentaries, converged upon Boeing Field in Seattle to celebrate the fiftieth anniversary of that remarkable plane. When these crewmen learned that Ed Wells, who had designed that plane when he was barely twenty-four years old, was on the field that day, they walked over to where he stood. A spokesman stepped forward and said, "We should all kneel down and kiss the ground you walk upon, Mr. Wells. We owe you so much for giving us that plane." The pilots were echoing from personal experience the conclusion of General Carl A. Spaatz, one of the top air commanders in United States military history, that "without the B-17, we might have lost the war."*

A year later, Wells lost a quiet, heroic battle with cancer, and those same pilots asked permission from his family to fly over in a B-17 during his memorial services and dip the plane's wings in the traditional military salute at "the loss of one of our own."

The Flying Fortress was only the first achievement in a remarkable career in aviation engineering. Knut Hammerskjold, Director-General of the International Air Transport Association, outlined the range of Wells' achievements when he presented Wells the Tony Jannus Award "for outstanding contributions to commercial aviation" in 1985. He took his listeners on a hypothetical flight and pointed out the retractable landing gear, the swept-wing configura-

---

*Quoted by Donald G. Sachs, an aviation history consultant and former B-17 pilot, during a lecture tour in 1989–90.

1

tion, the wing-surface controls, the pressurized cabin, the suspended engine pods, and the retractable shock-absorbing landing struts, all innovations perfected by Wells. The Flying Fortress, the B-29 Superfortress, and the Boeing 707, 747, 757, and 767 are all part of Wells' legacy.

What motivated this special man? There is a family story that when he was a child, our younger sister Peggy expressed a craving for something seen in a store window. Our mother responded, "But we don't have the money." The child offered an easy solution, "That's all right—just write a check." The Wells children never forgot our mother's stern injunction, "It's a serious crime to write a check unless you're sure you have money in the bank, and that applies to everything you do, my child."

This "money in the bank" motto was deeply engraved. We children learned early that one must be certain of facts before expressing an opinion; that one must do one's homework before taking action; and that bragging and boasting are heinous sins.

This strict standard was carried over with no deviation during Ed's tenure with the Boeing Company. Bill Jury, Boeing's Aerospace Division director, recalled after Ed's death that during his career with the company "he was considered to be 'Mr. Integrity' and, because of his example, that standard of his somehow permeated throughout the whole company. He was constantly urging, 'Let's not offer a plane until we can be sure it will be a good one.'"

During his lifetime Wells was heaped with honors. He was written about in scores of magazines and newspapers, but he always maintained his own standards of worth. If he was overpraised he would promptly set the record straight, refusing credit for the ideas and achievements of others.

Edward Curtis Wells was born August 26, 1910, the first child of the family to be born in a hospital. At the time there was a choice of two hospitals in Boise, Idaho. Our parents, of strong Methodist loyalty, were skeptical of both, since St. Luke's was sponsored by the Episcopal Church and St. Alphonsus was definitely Roman Catholic. The family was touchy about saints of any persuasion, but at least Luke was mentioned in the Bible, while Alphonsus was not.

Edward's three sisters were promised a look at him if we would walk responsibly the mile or more to the hospital. Upon reaching Mother's bedside, after gulping the odious odors of ether and disinfectant pervading hospital corridors in those days, we bent over

The Wells home in Boise

the ten-pound baby apprehensively, looking for any sudden change in coloring. We remembered that two years before, a little sister—"a blue baby"—had died a few hours after birth. Our doctor, Jack Springer, assured ten-year-old Mildred, my six-year-old twin, Alice, and me that our brother was indeed hale and hearty and "you must take good care of him because he's so important to your father."

Actually, Dr. Springer had enjoyed twitting Father for a short while (it was deemed unseemly in those days for a father to witness a birth), saying at first, "Congratulations, my friend, your wife has just given birth to a fifth daughter." Then, after a hearty guffaw, he announced a son had been born.

Our father was no male chauvinist. Certainly unusual to the times, he had since the honeymoon days shared in the housework without apology, provided that he could hang up his apron before answering the doorbell. However, he had expressed his longing for a son as the fulfillment of his dreams. When this baby had grown to manhood he would receive this letter on his birthday: "Tomorow you will be twenty-one. I was a very proud man that August morning when I walked down the street, trying to get used to the fact that I was the father of a son."

When he was ten days old, Edward Curtis was taken home to an unusual household arrangement. Our mother, ever anxious to better the family fortunes, had filled all the bedrooms of the house with "paying guests." There may have been many boarding or

Left: Laura Wells

Below left: Edward Lansing Wells

Below right: Ed at age one, in 1911, with his grandfather, Harrison Curtis Wells, in Huron, South Dakota

rooming houses in Boise at the time, but they were not run by families with young children. It was not considered safe or genteel to have such an arrangement.

Somehow Mother managed to give us a very normal private life amid this crowded situation. She supervised the building of two-story sleeping porches on the rear and one side of the house. These were to give her children strong lungs filled with good Idaho air, and also to protect us from the influences of the roomers. Although these porches were fitted with roll-down canvas curtains, Idaho winter storms taught us to cope, by scooping snow from the canvas bedspreads and snuggling next to flannel-wrapped hot bricks under the comforters.

Our household rules were strict, allowing no deviation on the part of the children or the roomers: no fraternization with the tenants; no conversations beyond polite answers to questions; no acceptance of gifts or favors; no gossip about what may or may not have been heard or seen; never any visits inside the rented rooms; and no use by the children of the upstairs bathroom (the only one with a tub) except for Saturday night baths, when that bathroom became off limits to the roomers.

A motley series of renters came and went during a ten-year period. Among them were a divorced mother and her handsome twelve-year-old son, Charles Farrar, who later became commandant of the Marine barracks at Quantico; Addison T. Smythe, a congressman representing Idaho; Lulu Fairbanks, a vivacious blonde who abandoned teaching to become a well-publicized newspaperwoman in Seattle; a YWCA executive secretary who was raped and murdered in a Boise alley; and a woman we named the "mad prisoner," who had to be restrained and committed to the Idaho State Hospital in Blackfoot.

While the children's bedrooms were the "air-conditioned" sleeping porches, our parents slept in a pull-down bed in a quasi-bedroom off the dining room, always referred to as "the study." The study walls were crowded by add-on bookcases with magic foldaway glass doors. Mother put every penny she could squeeze out of the rent money from the rooms into monthly payments for subscription books. Baby Ed slept on a trundle bed in the study bedroom until he was a year old, after which he graduated to a sleeping porch space of his own.

Our mother was six years older than our father, although family friends found it hard to believe. She started her adult life with a brief try as a country schoolteacher but didn't last out the nine-month contract, deciding she was not cut out to cope with unruly children. She was an artist and a creator at heart. After an apprenticeship with the famous Gage Brothers hatmakers in Chicago, she became one of their traveling "trimmers," sent here and there throughout the Midwest as temporary help to locally owned millinery stores. Among her assignments were West Point, Nebraska, where she picked up a little spoken German, and Huron, South Dakota, where she left the Chicago firm and set up her own millinery business in partnership with a woman friend.

A tall, willowy, beautiful woman, Mother used her creative imagination and deft fingers to take a piece of silk or satin and a feather or a flower and quickly stitch them into a work of art. In Huron, she met Edward Lansing Wells, who was beginning a career in the National Weather Service. Their first encounter apparently was an unpleasant one because he had placed her name without permission as a participant in a church group program. He later admitted to being an admirer of her "spunk" and the fact that she was conducting a successful business on her own. He fell madly in love, with a devotion that persisted throughout their sixty-year marriage.

During the years we children were at home, we never suspected that our parents ever disagreed. In later years Ed would testify that no child could ever wheedle a change of the decision of one parent by appealing to the other. And it was many years later that we realized that our parents had seldom agreed about anything. When Ed was to be married, Father wrote him these words of advice and explanation:

> No two people who have minds of their own will always agree about everything; to disagree without violation of love and confidence is an art that all married couples must learn if heartbreak is to be avoided. It is an open secret in this family, now that you all are grown, that your Mother and I have not always agreed, but I think you will realize that never in all the years has a grain of bitterness been left by our disagreements.

Edward Curtis received his middle name and possibly his tendency toward strong convictions about nonviolence from his paternal grandfather, Harrison Curtis Wells. Harrison's ancestors included some notable dissenters. One signed the death warrant of Charles I of England during the Civil Wars, and another was burned at the stake as the first Protestant martyr in the reign of "Bloody Mary." One ancestor fled to America as a Huguenot, forced out of France at the Revocation of the Edict of Nantes, but most of our ancestors became strict Seventh-Day Baptists in Rhode Island in the 1700s. Some remained in that faith, but Harrison and his immediate relatives became Methodists.

Harrison served as an orderly during the Civil War, caring for the wounded. Ed's grandmother, Zipporah Elizabeth Burdick Wells, died of what was probably muscular dystrophy when her son was five. Harrison Wells and Edward Lansing moved into a sod shanty on the South Dakota prairie, where they made a futile effort at farming. With no guns allowed in the house or in the hand, the two lived on a meager, unbalanced, largely carbohydrate diet. Eggs and butter were sold to provide necessary cash. One of Edward's jobs was to bring in his father's oxen at night. One night the little boy could not find the animals before dark, and wandered the prairie until he spotted the candle in the window of the shanty and followed it home. His father helped pull the thorns from Edward's bare feet and put him to bed in the top bunk. During the night the exhausted child rolled out of bed onto the floor, causing a back injury that plagued him the rest of his life, leaving him increasingly stooped.

Edward Lansing was passed around to various, more or less willing, relatives for the few months of winter schooling. Then, almost sight unseen, Harrison married an Irish girl who had been brought to America during the Potato Famine. He explained the marriage as "a need to have a woman in the house to look after the little boy." It was a strange relationship.

When Edward was ready for high school the three moved to Huron. During his sophomore year he was forced to quit school due to a severe eye inflammation which threatened to blind him. His regret over his missed education was the primary reason for the "study," the only sizable library in our neighborhood. Mother scarcely knew what she was buying, but she listened eagerly to the pitches of traveling salesmen and purchased volumes ranging from collections of fairy tales to Kant's *Critique of Pure Reason*, Darwin's *Origin of Species*, and Adam Smith's *Wealth of Nations*. We had a full set of Shakespeare, all of Dickens, and poetry by Longfellow, Whittier, Bryant, Wordsworth, Shelley, Byron, and Lowell. Edward used Bible histories and concordances to prepare for a popular Bible history class he taught for young nurses, teachers, and stenographers. And, in this Methodist family, the bookshelves also held a colorfully decorated volume on the life of Buddha titled *The Light of Asia*, possibly the gift of some well-meaning friends.

Although he often complained that some of the material was over his head, Father loyally read every word of that library, for he could not let his wife down when she had worked so hard to make the material available. As a result of that reading and the lifelong search for knowledge that it stimulated, he became, in the words of his son, "the best educated man I have ever known." The eye problem recurred periodically, but after a week or two of rest he was able to return to his books.

Young Ed learned to walk and talk at a very early age. Having mastered walking, he started to experiment by whirling around the room with his arms spread wide. This ended in disaster. One day, while Mother was making up the Daveno pull-down bed in the study, Ed whirled into the room. His extended left hand was caught in the closing hinges of the bedstead. The end of the ring finger was severed. Quickly Mother swaddled the bleeding hand in a roll of cheesecloth. With the baby bundled into a blanket, Mother, Alice, and I ran the three blocks to the trolley line. In 1911 we had no horse and buggy, no automobile, just a public streetcar three blocks from home.

When we arrived at Dr. Springer's office he asked, "Where's the end of the finger? Perhaps I can suture it on." In the excitement, no one had thought to look for it. Thus Ed went through life with what he considered to be only a minor cosmetic problem: a fingernail that protruded out of the end of the shortened ring finger on his left hand.

Ed talked clearly except for the pronunciation of any "r" sound, for which he invariably substituted "l." Our maternal grandmother, Sarah Wolfe Long, decided to take this matter in hand. For hours he sat on her lap, playing with a gold pocket watch on its gold chain while she attempted to teach him to say "the rat ran over the roof of the house with a piece of raw, red liver in its mouth." If he insisted upon "the lat lan over the loof of the house with a piece of law, led livel in its mouth," she would hide the watch in her pocket and he would be forced to try again. Success finally crowned her determination to "make him say it right."

Sarah Long was a resilient and determined individual, and there seems little doubt that these traits were an important inheritance which showed up strongly in Ed's adult life. In her widowhood she lived on eight dollars per month from her pension as a Civil War widow. Her husband had been an open-handed cosigner on other people's obligations, and among her possessions was a shoebox full of records of property lost through foreclosure or nonpayment of taxes. When she was nearing her eightieth year, she learned that the United States government was giving away Idaho desert sagebrush land, 160 acres of it, to veterans and veterans' widows just for laying claim and promising to live on the land for a certain number of years.

Sarah Long

Here was her El Dorado. She abandoned her home and friends in Iowa to come out "to be near Laura and her babies." Her desert land lay about ten miles from Caldwell, Idaho, which is roughly thirty miles from Boise. But there was an interurban trolley to Caldwell, and rides could be begged from other settlers for the rest of the way to the farm. Sarah knew well that irrigation water would never be available to her land in her lifetime. But it was promised, and now she would be able to leave something valuable to her children when she died. So she had barrels of water brought to her small ranch from the nearby Snake River. She boiled it to make it safe to drink and she strained it. She finally got a cistern in which to store it. She whacked the rampant rattlesnakes with her garden hoe; she built sagebrush smudge fires to rid herself of mosquitoes outside her house and flying ants within; she cursed the coyotes who tried to raid her chicken house at night. And she welcomed her sons-in-law who generously gave part of their annual vacations to grub sagebrush on her ranch as an aid to her "proving up on her land." Not long after her death in 1913, the water did come in abundance to irrigate her acres, and, as her Bible had promised, "the desert shall rejoice and blossom as the rose." Her very fertile wind-blown loess soil yielded (some time after her heirs sold it) wealth beyond her wildest dreams.

Ed Wells and his sisters retained pleasant memories of their visits to her ranch and never could forget her oft-used or oft-quoted "old saws": "Make your head save your heels" when a child did something stupid; and, if a child insisted upon pig-headedness, "If you are bound and determined to sit on a hot stove, you'll be sure to burn your arse good."

About one block from the Wells home in Boise lived Mother's sister Lily (or Lillie or Lillian, depending upon her mood). She and her husband, Hans Jorgen Roan, were a childless couple who could be depended upon for all the goodies that our parents could not afford. Somehow these gifts were provided with such tact and wisdom that jealousy and false pride never raised their ugly heads. Tickets to the circus were always mentioned as extras that Uncle Hans had been given; rides in the buggy behind "old Nellie" were offered because an errand in the country had to be made; and toys could be paid for by a modest task the child could perform. Uncle Hans, who called small Ed "Uncle's little man," hired a mechanic to fashion a small seat to be mounted between the handlebars of his bicycle so he could pedal Ed to see the trains come in and to see the trolley lines that ringed the town—the Yellow Belt Line, which Ed called the "Jello Belt Line."

When Ed was about three, he embarked upon his first automobile ride, taking him and his sisters half way across the state of Idaho. It happened in this way. Mother began to wear those strange uniforms of impending motherhood, those gowns of heavy material called "Mother Hubbards," that hung in pleats straight to the floor from the bustline. Since this indicated that another expected or, more probably, unexpected baby was due in the Wells family, it was decided to get us out of the house until after the birthing. A trip must be planned.

In May 1913, therefore, Uncle Hans bought an Overland roadster and outfitted it for the trip across the state to a sheep camp at Ketchum, a spot which later became the famous Sun Valley resort. The Roan and Wells families were devoted to camping, even in the horse-and-buggy days, and this location, owned by friends in the sheep-raising business, was the most cherished of all.

Ed at age three

The turtleback cover was removed from the little roadster in order to fasten in its place a spring-wagon seat. A fat bedroll was placed upon this seat and a rope handrail was installed to hold in the passengers and to provide a safer ride. Ed wanted to sit out in the wind on the bedroll, but was told he must sit snugly between Lily and Hans up in front, while Hans did the driving, except during those times when Lily had to steer the little car while the rest of the crew valiantly pushed the vehicle up places too steep to be managed by engine power alone. We three girls bounced along on the bedroll as the burdened car left Boise on that bright May morning amid taunts hurled at us by pedestrians on the sidewalks: "Get a horse! You'll never make it. Never. Never."

But make it we did, although by the slimmest of margins. A steering rod snapped and the car, out of control, jumped a small irrigation ditch, throwing Alice out onto the grassy meadow. A ranchman's forge came to the rescue to put the rod into usable shape again. Later, several tires blew out and the little car stood helpless along the road until rubber repairs could be made with a vulcanizer kit. When the car ran out of fuel, Hans and Lily bought a gallon of gas from a sympathetic fellow trekker and siphoned it from his car to ours. While they went into the Ketchum post office to ask for mail, we children left in the little roadster were scared out of our wits when a tire exploded under us. We had seen shoot-'em-up Westerns, and Ketchum seemed the right place for a gunfight. When the adults rushed out to the car, we all were screaming, "We didn't do it! Honest, we didn't." Ed never forgot the trip. It may well have been the start of his lifelong passion for automobiles and everything related to the transportation world.

When we returned from Ketchum we found a baby sister, Margaret Laura, soon called Peggy, beginning to take her turn in the trundle bed in the study.

Laura Wells was a loving mother but a strict disciplinarian. She would not tolerate a spoiled child, and her methods of training could be severe. Children who persisted in misbehavior (and we were usually given one chance to mend our ways) would be taken into the small lavatory downstairs and walloped with a razor strop or a thin rubber syringe hose or a lilac switch we had to select from the hedge in the back yard. Sometimes we were given a choice of weapons. She would punish the miscreant "until you stop crying." In later years we all found we could become very teary over gestures of kindness or sentiment, but in the presence of genuine crisis or loss or disappointment we were dry-eyed and strong.

The Wells family when Ed was about four. Back row, from left: Mary, Mildred, Alice; Edward Lansing holding Edward Curtis, Laura holding Margaret

Father's methods of discipline were quite different and more effective. Ed recalled that his father whipped him upon just a few occasions, but all the girls said he never laid a hand on them. Perhaps this was because he had such firm beliefs that no man should ever touch a woman in violence. His discipline was stern, but caring. For misbehavior, Ed would often recall, Father would take a child alone into the study, grasp the upper left arm firmly, and look with anguish at the one who had betrayed his trust. No child could for long stand that distressed accusation. Father set high standards of behavior for himself and for all those around him at work and at home, and his children were taught that less than the best achievement was unworthy of them.

Ed, at age five, perhaps forgot his mother's stern disciplinary ideas when he had words with an old woman in the neighborhood. Her house sat upon a corner lot where small children and older bicyclists made deep tracks across her well-manicured lawn as they short-cutted their travels. In defense of her grass, she erected a pipe barrier across that corner. Unfortunately, this made the area more attractive, giving the little children a chance to swing upon the iron bars, using them as playground equipment. Ed was among these children. When she threatened him with a broom, he spoke rudely to her. Consequently Mother received an angry phone call. She asked Ed if he was sorry for what he had done. He said, "No. She is a mean old lady." Laura then responded very characteristically, "If you refuse to say you are sorry, I shall not force you to tell a lie, but I am going to march you down to her house and you are going to tell her that Mrs. Wells is ashamed of her son for having been rude to a lady."

It was also when Ed was five that he took his first train ride and saw his first airplane. Since the farm portion which Mother had inherited from her mother's sagebrush claim was now seeded in a hay crop, the Wells exchequer was eased enough so that Mother, young Ed, and our little sister Peggy could visit relatives and do some sightseeing. Ed recalled the trip in 1985, when he spoke at ceremonies commemorating the fiftieth anniversary of the first flight of the famous Boeing Model 299:

> My first sight of an airplane was back in the days of the barnstorming period of aviation, when I was barely five years old. I received a very special treat: a trip by train from our home in Boise, Idaho, to San Francisco, to see the 1915 World Fair. For a youngster who at the time was sure he wanted to be a locomotive engineer, this trip was quite a thrill, over-

shadowed only by the things seen at the fair. None of these was more impressive, however, than the first view of an airplane in flight, piloted by the renowned stunt flier, Lincoln Beachey. After the fair and the long train trip home, my interest in aviation became dormant, as there were few barnstormers in that part of the country, and I was soon busy entering grade school.

Ed had taught himself to read when he was four years old by persistent questioning: "What does that say?" The family was unaware of his accomplishment until suddenly one day, as the child was sprawled out above the newspaper on the floor, he announced, "The Germans have sunk another ship in the Atlantic." Stunned, someone asked, "How do you know?" He grinned, "It says so right here."

Young Ed's precocious ability in reading was a delight to his Uncle Hans. Sunday afternoons in the Roan household were given over to reading the Sunday supplement's weekly chapter of *The Perils of Pauline*. The reading aloud was alternated between Hans and Lily, but Ed begged to join in. They had him read *Pigs Is Pigs* and *Penrod and Sam*. Ed and Hans would start to giggle as Ed read the preposterous humor in *Pigs Is Pigs*, and often they would be doubled up until the giggling fits could subside.

A year later, when Ed had started to school, his first teacher begged Mother to stop the boy from any more learning "until the other children can catch up." She retorted that "I could as easily stop the water from going over the falls at Niagara as I could stop that boy from learning."

We children had few toys in comparison to the affluent children across the street, where there was an entire room of the house devoted to playthings. Among these were working models of steam engines that young Ed coveted; building blocks that could reproduce a cathedral; and a complete set of the famous Schoenhut Circus of wooden clowns and animals with grooves cut into the soles of their feet so they could be made to balance on ladders and stools and could stand on top of one another.

Our toys, such as they were, had to be kept in what was always referred to as "the playhouse," an old outhouse whose pits had been filled in with fresh-smelling dirt and boarded over. The backyard play area was tiny, because most of the space was given over to the woodshed, the chicken house, the vegetable garden, and the fruit trees, all necessary to keep food upon the table. Thus, we were forced to be inventive if we were to have any toys at all.

Father greatly admired people who were skillful with their hands, since he had little manual dexterity of his own. Mother, on the other hand, had her immense millinery skills and could wield a hammer or manage a saw as easily as she could her needle and her aged sewing machine. From an early age, Ed loved tools and used them well.

When Ed was five, he and I decided we could build ourselves an automobile large enough for both of us to ride in. Scrounging around, we found wheels from the twins' baby carriage, which had finally been demoted to hauling sagebrush down on the farm. Mother gave us a discarded broomstick for a steering column and a wooden disk (her wig-mold in the millinery trade) for a steering wheel. A grocer provided orange crates for the chassis. Two salmon cans from the family trash barrel were salvaged for headlights. The car was painted black (Aunt Lily's contribution) with yellow stripes. The word PACKARD was boldly emblazoned across the front, where a radiator could be imagined. All it needed to reach perfection was a motor. Ed thought if we could just find a discarded tricycle front wheel with pedals intact, we could power the vehicle with ease.

Our fervent prayers were answered. Crossing a vacant lot on our way home from downtown, we found the wheel abandoned upon a trash heap. But joy was short-lived. We had not reckoned with our parents' strict moral code. "Where did you get that wheel and to whom does it belong?" The answer was easy, "It doesn't belong to anyone." The parents' rejoinder was swift, "And certainly not to you."

No picking fruit off abandoned trees, no sneaking candy in the grocer's store, no tricycles off dump heaps. We children could not even have the worn-out government box-kites used to measure temperatures and winds aloft for the Weather Bureau. (Actually, by government fiat, these had to be burned when they no longer were fit for government use.) And we could not play around with those fascinating snowshoes that Father sometimes had to use on his winter inspection trips of Idaho weather stations.

The question of moral values also arose with leisure activities and games. Our Methodist parents adhered to church standards of no dancing, no drinking of alcohol, no card games (with a few exceptions), no playing of billiards, and, for many years, no attendance at stage plays or motion picture presentations. This didn't leave much for children to participate in except Sunday School picnics, Christmas programs, and parties where children were limited

Ed on a hike at nine or ten

to playing "drop the handkerchief" or "post office" or "spin the bottle." Certain card games, however, were allowed in the family circle, games like Flinch and Rook, because these had "no spots." Checkers were encouraged, but chess was always a question mark. Then, one Christmas, someone gave us an item called "A Game Board," a square about the size of a card table with reversible sides and many game possibilities.

What fun, what endless invention was held out with that board. But first, some gambling temptations had to be removed: the cue sticks had to be broken and burned and the string nets had to be cut out of the corner pockets.

The one activity we all cherished was hiking in the hills. Father was an avid hiker, and each Sunday afternoon he chose a child to accompany him on his exploration of the foothills surrounding Boise. Ed looked forward to the chance to see the bloodhounds on leash being exercised along the paths above the Idaho State Penitentiary on the slopes of Table Rock, or to make the steep climb up the spine of Camel Back where he could shiver over the possibilities of falling down the basalt chute called "Devil's Slide." On these afternoon hikes, Ed and we girls were often taught to memorize some of the classic poetry which our father dearly loved.

In spite of the lack of money and the taboos, life was exciting for

Ed and his family. There were so many things to be tried, so much to be learned, so much to be created. During his sixth and seventh years, Ed began filling tablets with designs, with sketches of trains, trolleys, boats, and automobiles, some of which he remembered seeing, others of which sprang from pure imagination. He tried to experiment a bit with drawing airplanes. He built many models, crude at first, and conducted experiments, usually safe, supervised, and successful.

Then everything took a new turn. Father was appointed meteorologist in charge of the United States Weather Bureau office in Portland, Oregon. To Boise folks in general, Portland represented fulfillment, heaven, the brass ring.

2

The Education of an Engineer

Father went ahead of the family in January 1919 to report to his new assignment as head of the Weather Bureau office in Portland and to pick out a house. His only regret was being separated from Laura for their wedding anniversary.

Much would be left behind in Boise, although not a great deal in the way of material possessions, because the family seldom threw anything away. But left behind would be "the paying guests." With the sale of the farm property and the Boise home, and with Father's promotion, we could at last have a house entirely our own. Father described it in his letter from Portland:

> There are three large bedrooms with walk-in closets big enough in which to add a cot; a study; a living room with built-in bookcases and a fireplace; a dining room; a large kitchen with adjoining pantry; and a semifinished basement with indoor clotheslines, stationary washtubs, a coal-burning furnace and a workbench so that young Ed can have the time of his life, building anything his young hands can manage.

Left behind, also, was the routine of steamy Monday washday, with the dozen or more bedsheets hanging to dry in a white labyrinth around the kitchen or back porch on days of inclement weather. Gone, too, would be the routine Saturdays when that kitchen was redolent with the fumes of hot lard as Mother fried dozens and dozens of doughnuts, an idea she had suggested to the twins and Ed "as a means of helping out on the war effort by putting money into Liberty Bonds so you can all go to college." We girls bagged the doughnuts and, with Ed pulling the little red wagon, we went out every Saturday to peddle our wares at fifty cents a dozen, feeling that we could not bear to come home until all had been sold. On some lucky days we were able to deliver as many as two hundred or three hundred doughnuts to some gala church function where a whole congregation might be in a doughnut-dunking mood. Mother never charged for her devoted labor, but "to make the children responsible" we had to reimburse her for every ounce of flour, sugar, and lard. Ed was in charge of the arithmetic for this accounting.

Without regret, we turned over to the new owners the despised chore of the chickens, the gathering of the eggs, the cleaning the muck from the chicken house. But with a great deal of regret we bestowed upon the milk deliveryman the only pet we ever owned (except Mother's canaries, who always died). He was a water spaniel who couldn't swim a stroke.

To Portland would go all the accumulated family furniture, including an amazing rocking chair upon whose leather seat was tooled a sinking battleship ringed with the words "Remember the Maine" and upon whose wooden back was carved in relief a battle scene of bombs bursting over Havana. And, of course, the precious books from the Boise study/library/bedroom would go to Portland, together with most of the family traditions.

Among these family traditions would be the blue enameled "tithe box" which always had a hallowed place upon our parents' dresser top. Laura and Edward Wells had early made a vow to give one-tenth of any earned income to church or charity and this vow was kept inviolate throughout their marriage. At the time of the move, they decided that we children had reached the age where we too could be trusted with the money in the blue box. (And, lest any child be tempted to cheat, Father kept meticulous books on this fund.) Change could be made out of the money in the box, where the tithe money was always kept in cash. Borrowing from the box for any especially dire emergency was allowed, provided the borrower would sign an IOU to be placed beneath its legs. Somehow we conceived the idea that "an all-seeing eye" hovered above the box to keep us honest.

To Portland, also, would come the lifelong insistence of the parents upon family prayers following breakfast. A portion of the King James Bible was read, with Mother and Father alternating in the reading, after which the family would kneel down in front of the chairs. As an adult, Ed could never understand the push for "modern versions" of the Bible in the vernacular because in his early years he had become so used to the mellifluous flow of the Shake-

spearean wording and rhythm of the King James Version. He had
found it to be warm and as understandable as the words of a foreign language well learned and loved.

Two other traditions went along to the new home. One was the
celebration of Harrison Wells' birthday with a serving of strawber-
ry shortcake and thick cream, even though our grandfather had
been dead for years. The second tradition was the Sunday night
gathering of the family in the new study where chocolate topped
with marshmallows was served, while Father (a would-be actor)
read aloud from the classics or recited from Shakespeare or "Evangeline" or "Hiawatha," or something else that caught his fancy. Ed
could still, in adulthood, imagine a shiver at the memory of his father's slender fingers approaching him as he recited from *Hamlet*,
"I am thy father's ghost, doomed to haunt thee . . ." Some Sunday
nights ended with a family songfest around the piano, belting out
gospel songs of "Amazing Grace," "Deep River," or (Father's favorite) "Don't Yah Hear Dem Bells," remembered from his bache-
lor days when he sang in a male quartet. The piano had come into
the Wells family home when Aunt Lily had entered one of those
contests where the letters of a commercial logo are made into the
greatest number of words possible. She slaved over all the diction-
aries she could amass, and the piano for the Wells children was her
reward.

Since the family could seldom throw anything away, another
family "totem" was brought to Portland. It seems that when I was
nine months old, I had brushed death with a virulent attack of
pneumonia. I had turned blue and the family physician had given
up. Someone in the neighborhood suggested a spoonful of whiskey. Even though the family was a fiercely teetotaling clan, the
whiskey was bought and the two teaspoons (or tablespoons?) of it
were forced down my throat, and because of it, or in spite of it, I
survived. The bottle was recorked and placed upon the back recesses of the highest cupboard shelf in the kitchen, perhaps as a good
luck charm. And there it sat, untasted but unquestioned, in the
back recesses of the highest cupboard in every house we lived in
thereafter, a liquor untouched by human lips for fifty years. When
our parents retired to California, I finally poured the whiskey down
the kitchen sink drain.

The house needed some work, and the task of paint scraping and
sanding was assigned as a job for everyone. Mildred, the oldest
daughter, escaped the chore because she was already attending
Willamette University, that "oldest school west of the Mississippi"

of Methodist aegis "where children will be under a good influence" (so parents firmly believed).

The paint situation in the Portland house was its main drawback, possibly the reason it had been sold at a discounted price. A previous owner had brushed a thin coat of white enamel over dark brown varnished walnut wood, causing the woodwork to have a leprous look. This had to be removed. Ed was only eight years old, but, along with the rest of the family, he went at the task with a will.

When summer was over, Ed began classes at Rose City Park School, only a few blocks away on a steep hill. But the speed with which he managed his homework assignments left him plenty of time to experiment with constructing things at the crude workbench in the home basement. His tools were limited: a crosscut saw, as well as a clawhammer and small coping saw his mother bought for him, a screwdriver or two, and a small hand drill. With a birthday check he managed to supplement these with a small soldering iron and a bit of solder. He began to make simple steam engines from his mother's discarded tin cans. These became more sophisticated and eventually good enough to power his various Meccano creations. When the small power plants did not work to suit him he sometimes crushed them in a fit of frustration, for he had a consuming need to make things work. In later years he had learned so well to control this temper that adult friends would scarcely believe he had ever had one.

When Ed was nine, his father gave him a book called *Model Making*, which he treasured throughout his life. In the front of the book his father had written:

> All your life you have taken the keenest delight in building. Someday your life will find expression in some real contribution to the advance of the world in something material that you have built. But not alone in wood and stone and iron and brass are enduring structures built. The building of a character is the greatest achievement of all, and in this I am expecting you to excel.

Perhaps Ed Wells' own words, during an interview with Donald Schmechel about a year before he died, explain his avid interest in building things:

> My dad had a great influence upon me. I think both my mother and my father realized that I had an interest in scientific things quite early in my life. I always liked to draw pictures, particularly pictures of trains and

boats and cars. Not airplanes at that time, however. But my parents encouraged my drawing. We were not overly endowed with material goods so that there were many things that we were not able to have because we were a large family and in modest circumstances. My dad in particular would encourage my interest by furnishing me with books.

Father no longer had time for the treasured hikes with his children, but Ed made friends with two neighbor brothers with whom he could hike and explore the beauty and the mysteries of the Portland woods. The three boys were especially attracted to the stony recesses of a place called Rocky Butte, at that time on the far eastern outskirts of the city. Atop that butte, which rises abruptly and steeply out of the flatlands, a boys' military school stood on one side and on the other a constant, rat-a-tat-tat of jackhammers cut out stone in an active quarry. Down at the base of the butte in a natural grotto, Catholic builders had constructed a sanctuary in honor of the Virgin Mary. The three boys often peered in with awe and fascination at the garishly painted statues and the flickering lights of the votive candles. Upon several occasions they apparently talked of "snitching" one of the votive lights to illuminate the treehouse they had built in the woods on a vacant lot near their homes. But for Ed, perhaps the deterrent was a vision of his mother's taking him, if caught, before the Pope at Rome to make him say, "Mrs. Wells is ashamed of her young son and his felonious behavior."

The people most missed in the move from Boise were Hans and Lily, who had provided the extras in our lives with such love and finesse. Now the goodies had to be sent to Portland by mail or the void filled by eager messages over the telephone. In the summer of 1920, however, when Ed was almost ten, an invitation and tickets arrived, asking me to chaperone Ed and Peggy to Boise by train for a short stay that would include a hunting, fishing, and camping trip once more to the sheep camp at Sun Valley. Ed was ecstatic at the prospect of another trip aboard a train.

While we were in Boise, Uncle Hans decided that the two younger children should be taught to swim. He persuaded me to take them every day for two weeks to that famous geothermally heated pool that Boise has always lovingly called "The Nat" (Natatorium of the City of Boise). The sulphurous damp smell pervading the old wooden structure was otherworldly. The steep slides at the sides of the great steaming water and the trapezes hung perilously overhead were exciting to contemplate. The swimming instructor turned Ed into a skilled swimmer, which brought pleasure to him for a lifetime.

That year, when Ed returned home to Portland, he decided to build himself a small violin. He began with a discarded cigar box, but that soon proved unfeasible. After this failure, he procured better pieces of wood that could be whittled, sanded, carved, and bent into shape for a good, playable violin. When Uncle Hans saw the remarkable finished product, he bought Ed a Guarnerius, or at least a very expensive violin which bore the signature of Guarnerius. Young Ed finally convinced his family that he had no desire to become a violinist—he just wanted to see if he could build one. The expensive instrument was returned to the seller with the refund put away for Ed's college fund.

For the Christmas of Ed's tenth year he wanted very much to give his parents a worthy gift. He decided upon a small pirate ship of his own design that could grace the fireplace mantel. Lacking money for supplies, he used wood scraps from an apple box. He laminated the layers of wood, then rasped, whittled, and sanded this into a proper hull. He begged from Mother corks, beads, and pieces of metallic Christmas wrapping paper with which to fashion ship's lights, and used matchsticks for porthole cannons. Coarse linen sewing thread made ratlines, shrouds, and struts to hold the masts in place. Mother that year had bought for a pittance an entire bolt of government war surplus airplane linen, out of which she could make suits, table linen, and other household necessities. Small scraps of this became the tiny ship's sails. After coating these with shellac, Ed borrowed a neighbor's vacuum cleaner and reversed the flow of air to dry the shellac and to make the small sails billow out stiff forever as in a strong breeze. When Uncle Hans saw the original model, he made Ed an offer of ten dollars for a duplicate for his mantel in Boise.

That same year Ed built his second airplane model, the first flyable one, and a model automobile of his own design. (His first aircraft model had been a neat little four-by-five-inch job he carved out of three pieces of wood, glued and fastened together with tiny tacks, when he was between six and seven years of age.) He made many models after this, for the most part of original designs, although some were fashioned to simulate planes used in World War I. According to Ed himself, his second plane was "whittled out of apple box wood in the basement of our Portland home, and launched with a good throw, it could glide fifty feet or so." The next plane was patterned after a flying boat, with a motor from a twisted

One of Ed's model planes

rubber band. The model automobile was a sporty little roadster slightly resembling a Stutz Bearcat. It was made of molded cardboard, painted a glossy gray and black, with wheels salvaged from a discarded carpetsweeper.

In his speech commemorating the 299, Ed described his first models:

> After the end of World War I, barnstorming again became more popular and model airplane kits began to become available for the various World War I types of airplanes. Quite often the local barnstormers used a "Jenny" or some modification of it. So my first model was quite naturally a flying model of the "Jenny." I couldn't afford the price of the construction kit, so, starting with the raw materials and some fairly simple drawings, I had to learn how to build the model from scratch. That was a lot of work, but hindsight tells me I learned a lot more about the fundamentals that way than I would have learned by assembling a kit.
>
> No one was more surprised than I was when the crude little replica of a "Jenny" actually flew—not far, to be sure—but it did fly! By this time I was quite sure I wanted to be an engineer (no longer a locomotive engineer) but I wasn't yet sure just what kind of an engineer. I continued to build models—airplanes, trains, automobiles and other mechanical marvels—without playing favorites.

In 1923 Ed started high school. Washington High School, to which he would normally have been assigned, had burned to the ground, so his first year was spent at Jefferson High School about five miles away. It was decided that he should obtain an afternoon paper route, but the only one available was in what was known as the Burnside District in the heart of Portland. After school each day Ed took the streetcar for almost five miles to downtown Portland to deliver his papers. He told Donald Schmechel:

> I picked up the papers and took them around to all of the business establishments, restaurants and a few places in the red light district. This was a kind of eye-opener for a kid thirteen or fourteen years old. Those establishments always paid their bills promptly. The worst customers for me getting paid were the banks. But this was a pretty good paper route because you could have a lot of customers in a fairly small area, walking the whole route without the need of a bicycle. I'm sure my folks did not know what kind of place my route was in, what with the prostitutes and the winos. Of course, I was pretty safe, because the winos didn't think I had a dime to spare, and the madams knew I didn't have a dime to spare, either.

During his sophomore year a new school, Grant High, was finished closer to home. For Ed high school was a breeze and he took pride in the new building. He was enrolled in a college preparatory course, Latin required, and French chosen as a fulfillment of the foreign language requirement. He and a high school pal, obviously bored with the French class, made the life of Madame Von Vincengarode constantly uneasy, because they took delight in stimulating the class to mischief as often as they dared, by surreptitiously passing romantic notes in French around the classroom. Apparently she was not the only teacher to be discomfited by Ed, because he later credited his physics teacher with "a pretty good tolerance for some of our experimental activities." This puckish behavior would have puzzled Ed's later friends at Boeing, although they sometimes mentioned the glint of humor in his eyes. Most thought of Ed, until they got to know him intimately, as being too well-mannered to have caused trouble anywhere.

Fortunately in high school Ed and about five other fellows with extremely high IQs were singled out by Omar Bittner, a math teacher who took them under his wing, deciding that they were worth encouraging and pushing. He offered them an exciting extracurricular course in calculus. They came to love both the subject and the teacher.

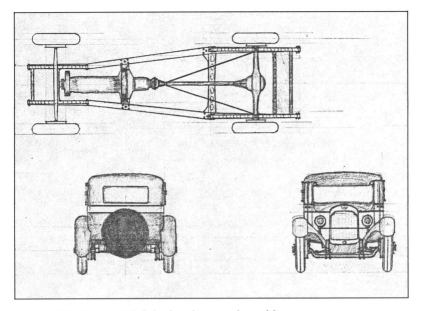

Automobile designs Ed did when he was about fifteen

In the third year of high school Ed seems to have acquired, at last, a second-hand bicycle to go to and from school, not always with a smooth ride according to a letter to his father, who was on a weather station inspection trip:

> I had a wreck on my bike the other day when I was going to school. I was going as fast as I could and the front forks turned on the handlebars and I took a spill. I tore my pants but mother fixed that. I bumped my side and I think I broke a rib. It is almost all right now, but it hurts if I press it. I guess I will have to quit going to the "Y" because it comes on Wednesday after school and on Saturday at 11 o'clock. I hope this letter is long enough for once.

Ed found time for extracurricular activities in addition to his paper route:

> I was on the staff of the high school newspaper and the annual. I don't know how that happened, because I can't recall having had any particular interest in writing at that time. I tried out for football once, but decided it wasn't for me. From then on, as far as athletics was concerned, I went out for track in the quarter-mile and the half-mile, although I wasn't very good at either. I was a little better at the half-mile.

He forgot to mention in this interview with Don Schmechel that he did earn a school sweater with a big "G" sewed upon it. His sister Peggy would have "given my eye teeth if he would have let me borrow it."

When time came for Ed's graduation from high school in 1927, he was expected to go to Willamette University as had his older sisters. There was an added reason for conformity: Father had now become a trustee of the institution and was proud of the honor. But Willamette had no engineering program. Since all the Wells children understood that the privilege of a college education depended on agreeing to contribute to the next child in line, I felt I had a vested interest in Ed's education. I proposed that if Ed would attend Willamette for two years that he then be allowed to transfer to the School of Engineering at Stanford. After a trip in the family's first car, a Dodge touring sedan, first to Willamette to evaluate the freshman and sophomore math and science courses and then to Stanford to mesh their requirements with Willamette's offerings, we mapped out a four-year schedule and got the schools to put it into writing. The trip, hurried because Ed had a summer job awaiting him in Portland, was made as quickly as possible on the tediously slow, tortuous, and bumpy roads of that day.

During the high school years Ed had worked on Saturdays at a hardware store a couple of blocks from home. "For twenty-five cents an hour, which wasn't all that bad in those days," he remembered. However, the summer job of 1927 was obviously better—a shipping clerk and delivery boy at Chanslor and Lyons Company, a large auto parts distributor in Portland. The pay was very modest and the hours long, but Ed would have been happy to have paid them for the thrill of working around automobiles if he had owned the funds.

Dorothy Ostlund Wells, who became his wife, recalled later that "never was Ed so happy as when he was working with something to do with automobiles. He spent his life designing airplanes, but he could never get his fill of cars, buying every automobile magazine that came on the stands, and talking interminably with his son about automobiles, new and old."

Chanslor and Lyons gave Ed the chance to know every car of that day and every part that made up each of them. Ed decided to make automotive engineering his career. As he told Schmechel:

My interest goes back to pre-college days, and, in fact, for three years in college my objective was a mechanical engineering degree and training suitable for automotive engineering.... Before and during college, I held jobs selling automotive parts and accessories, working in an automotive machine shop, working on instrument repairs and service, and working on the business and collection end of the operation. This direct contact with automotive activity generated an interest which has never entirely been forgotten.

Following the summer with Chanslor and Lyons, Ed entered Willamette University and became a member of the Phi Delta Theta fraternity. During the hazing part of his initiation, he was blind-folded and taken for a dizzying ride into the country. He blamed that experience for his later tendency to airsickness.

Ed seems to have enjoyed campus life and his studies at Willamette, especially his classes in mathematics. "It was a small school," he recalled later, "but it had an excellent faculty, particularly the professor of mathematics, a Professor Matthews." Here he could take all of the liberal arts required for graduation from Stanford and as much science and math as Willamette offered. He loaded his schedule but still found some time for extracurricular activities; he went out for track and debate.

The rules for conduct at Willamette were very strict, and upon at least one occasion Ed did run afoul of them. The school allowed no dancing, no liquor, no card playing, etc. Ed and three classmates were caught playing poker one night in the bell tower of the college chapel. Their flashlights had given them away. It was, for a time at least, a question of having to expel all four. However, after apologies were forthcoming, all was forgiven and the four could stay on. In later years when Ed, too, had become a trustee of Willamette University, he could grin and say, "Perhaps it helped that my dad was on the Board." Then, with a wider grin still, he would add, "I never could figure out whether our greatest sin was in playing poker, or in playing it in the sacred chapel tower."

During the summers of 1928–30, Ed worked for another auto parts distributor, known in Portland by the name of "W. E. Burns—Dan Burns, Not Brothers—The Same Man." Ed's title was "clerk and instrument repair salesman." He was in the Portland store during the summers, but during the Willamette semesters he worked for the Salem branch on Saturdays and other hours he could arrange. Much of their work was machining pistons for what was known as the Bach tri-motor plane for air transport up and down the West Coast by the Pacific Air Transport Company.

In the fall of 1929, Ed entered the School of Engineering at Stanford University. He realized that his going to Stanford would take great sacrifice on the part of his parents, plus hard work on his own part. In fact he had tried to transfer to Oregon State at the beginning of his sophomore year because it was closer to home and cheaper than Stanford, but he was unable to reconcile the two schools' different requirements. "Fortunately, it all worked out very well," he told Schmechel. "A factor which might have influenced me in going to Stanford was that it had not only an excellent engineering school, it had more of a requirement for liberal arts for engineering students than most other schools had."

Campus housing was scarce at Stanford, so Ed rented a room off campus in Palo Alto. Later there was an opening in Encino Hall, which was primarily a freshman dorm but which did allow space to some upperclassmen. In his senior year Ed lived in the Stanford Union and shared a room with a San Diego fellow, an avid railroad buff who shared Ed's interest in model trains.

There were other warm and lasting friendships made at Stanford. Ed joined a local church group and contacted some close friends of his parents in Palo Alto who were members of the church. Their house was a home away from home for him.

The engineering classes were challenging, and Ed found the assignments tough. Perhaps this was why he loved the school. Extracurricular activities, except for those social times on Sundays, did not fit into his rigorous schedule. "Just going to school and making the grades was a full-time job," he said, "and although the school was not a large one, it was bigger than I was used to, so I had a lot of catching up to do."

Several professors were influential. Ed was especially grateful to those who taught students how to study and who showed them the essentials in engineering. One of these was the professor teaching Theory of Elasticity, Ed told Schmechel, "I've always had an ambition to get an 'A' from one of Professor Jacobsen's courses and I got it for my final grade—they're notably scarce from him."

The engineering curriculum laid out for Ed on that trip to the campus in 1927 worked out almost to the finest detail. Almost, but not quite. On the week before graduation in 1931, with his name already printed on the list of graduates with "great distinction" (Stanford's customary usage in place of *summa cum laude*), it was discovered that Ed was one-quarter of a credit short of the necessary score. The Wells family held its collective breath. Finally a letter came from Ed saying his graduation had been assured. The university authorities decided that this man, who had been awarded

Ed and his father, about 1931

membership in Phi Beta Kappa, Tau Beta Pi, and Blue Key, and was said to have earned the highest grades ever achieved in the engineering school with the exception of Herbert Hoover, who equaled him, should be allowed to graduate.

The week before that Stanford commencement, Ed could not contain his joy. It burst forth in this letter:

Dear Dad,

Here's a clipping from Friday's paper that may be quite a pleasant surprise to you and mother. I had almost made up my mind to keep it a secret and let you be surprised by seeing the news on the commencement program, but the news is too good to keep. It is an honor that I count almost above Phi Beta Kappa, since there are those in Phi Beta Kappa who are not included in the "great distinction" list. I haven't said much about it, but I have been holding my breath hoping to be included, yet fearing that for some reason I wouldn't be, for it really has been one of my first ambitions. I'm hoping it makes you half as happy as it makes me. Your loving son, Ed.

Ed finished college still unsure as to what kind of engineering he wanted to pursue. His career at Boeing began as happenstance. During his junior year at Stanford, the entire country was in the depths of the Great Depression. Jobs were very scarce and Ed badly needed a good job for the summer. "After three years towards a degree in mechanical engineering, Lady Luck stepped in, as she often does when least expected," he told Schmechel. "I was in dire need of a job for the summer of 1930—otherwise, I wouldn't have enough money to return to school in the fall. Those who were trying to finish college in the early '30s will remember exactly what I faced—jobs were scarce."

Ed had heard from friends in Portland that there might be a chance for work at the Boeing Company in Seattle. So during his spring break at Stanford, he headed north for an interview. In his hand he carried a portfolio of his drawings and in his pocket a glowing letter of recommendation from W. E. Burns—Dan Burns, Not Brothers—The Same Man. The Boeing people said there were no vacancies for summer jobs, but Ed asked if they would just look at a few drawings that he had brought along. They were impressed, telling him that he could work as an apprentice engineer if a job opened up in June. This seemed to be a very big "if," and Ed returned discouraged to Portland. In June news arrived that a Boeing engineer had been injured in an automobile accident. Ed was summoned on the strength of his drawings. That summer he became the only college student working in the Boeing Engineering Department.

In his interview with Donald Schmechel, Ed recalled this turning point in his life:

> This summer at Boeing, aviation had been my salvation, educationally, at least, and I suppose I should have seen the handwriting on the wall at that time. But I returned to school in the fall of 1930 without deciding in favor of aviation and began to send out employment applications for a great variety of mostly nonexistent jobs, including an application for so-called "permanent" employment at Boeing. And I had also sent an application for a place in the on-the-job training in automobile design at the Chrysler Corporation in Detroit.

Upon receiving his diploma, Ed began to hope for an offer of that "permanent job" at Boeing, but there seemed no openings available: "The company had been through a low point, so I took occasional employment anywhere I could find it, including a brief job on a surveying crew near Portland. Just when I was about to give up hope of getting a job at Boeing, I got word from them that a job was available and they asked me to report the following Monday, which, of course, I did. And that started me off on the rest of my career."

3

Seattle, Dorothy, and the Flying Fortress

Ed Wells boarded the train for Seattle and the new job almost dead broke but unencumbered. There had been a small romance during his high school days when he imagined himself enamored of a sloe-eyed, dark-haired neighbor girl with a Spanish name, a bit older than himself. She later remembered it as "a sweet puppy love."

After he went to Willamette University, he met another high school girl. She had boarded in the Wells home during a church convention while he was away at school. The only vacant bedroom was Ed's, and just as she was ready to say her goodbyes and thank-yous he arrived, unannounced, from Salem. She insisted upon making up the bed with fresh linen as a token of her appreciation of the Wellses' hospitality. To get Ed's attention, she short-sheeted his bed. A letter-writing campaign followed this episode. In the fall semester she enrolled in Willamette and when Ed transferred to Stanford, she enrolled in the University of California at Berkeley. With not a spare dime in Ed's college budget, commuting up the peninsula and across the bay to Berkeley raised a serious problem, and romancing by long distance telephone was just as restricted. In Ed's senior year, this girl found a Berkeley man and by mutual consent the romance with Ed withered on the vine.

He arrived in Seattle with two pieces of baggage: a small suitcase holding his few possessions and a bag of cheap golf clubs which had belonged to our father. When Ed was in high school Father had expressed a longing to try out a game of golf, so the family had pooled its limited resources to surprise him at Christmas. A few experimental holes were enough to convince Father that golf was not for him, but Ed turned out to be a "natural" with those same clubs and the game brought him lifelong enjoyment.

Ed was proudly wearing his first store-bought suit. Always before his clothes had been made by our mother, who was not only a competent milliner but an expert tailor. We girls became expert at ripping up the seams of our Uncle Hans's tailor-made discards, which Mother fashioned into Ed's "plus-fours" (golf-type knickers) that high school boys of that age wore.

In Ed's suitcase, along with his other clothes, was a treasure he cherished beyond gold: a small packet of letters held together with a wide rubber band. The letters represented just one more tradition in the Wells family. When the children began one by one to move out of the house, each one was assigned a day of the week upon which Father would write a letter to that child. Ed's day was Tuesday. We all knew that if the letter bearing the postmark of our assigned day did not arrive, Father was snowbound on a Weather Bureau inspection trip or flooded out or seriously ill. As a bonus each year, on our birthday would come a special letter and a poem expressing the love and pride he felt for us. On Ed's nineteenth birthday, just before he started for Stanford, Father wrote:

Swift the winged years have sped
Since that radiant August morn
Then as dawn the East o'erspread,
Came the news. "A son is born."

Never can the childless man
Know the surge of purest joy
Through my inmost soul which ran
As I beheld my newborn boy.

Nineteen years have come and gone,
Bringing changes as they fly;
You to stature full have grown;
Past the noon of life am I.

Yet, in spite of passing time,
Marking change for you and me,
Still remains the joy sublime,
Pride in what you've grown to be.

When I view the years ahead;
See the man you are to be;
Faith reveals the path you'll tread,
On to heights denied to me.

The model 40-A (*Boeing 3255B*)

Pride and joy akin to pain
O'er my soul come pouring in;
Pride in what you will attain;
Joy in victories you will win.

Thirty years later, he sent the same poem, with this comment: "Well, this may not have been good poetry, but in the years since then it has proved to be good prophecy. More power to you in the years to come!"

Ed's landlady from the summer before welcomed him back to her home on Beacon Hill. He settled in, eyeing with anticipation the commodious basement in her house that he hoped he could use for a shop.

On the first Monday in July 1931, Ed began his permanent assignment at Boeing. The company had received in March its biggest order in ten years, for 135 P-12E fighters, and its financial prospects seemed good despite the Depression.

Boeing had come a long way from modest beginnings. Fifteen years before, William E. Boeing had founded a small outfit called Pacific Aero Products Company. In 1917, having built a total of two

The Ox Bow factory, later known as the Red Barn (*Boeing P28*)

airplanes, the company settled in at Shipyard on the Duwamish and changed its name to The Boeing Airplane Company. Two young graduates from the University of Washington School of Engineering were hired: Clairmont L. Egtvedt and Philip Gustav Johnson. Johnson, age twenty-three, began working on detailed blueprints of rib and spar sections on a plane for which he coined the term "a stick-and-wire job." His genius was in tooling and production, however, and in 1922 he was promoted to vice president and general manager.

Most of Boeing's early contracts had been for military planes, but in 1926 the U.S. Post Office decided to turn airmail delivery over to private carriers. Boeing bid for the San Francisco to Chicago route, the longest in the world at that time, and won the contract with its Model 40A, which was designed to add revenues by carrying two paying passengers. It was Boeing's first major entry into commercial transport. Boeing Air Transport was organized in 1927 and set to work to build and put in service 25 Model 40As by July. The next year Boeing bought Pacific Air Transport and organized Boeing of Canada, Ltd. In 1929 the company bought National Air Transport to complete the service to New York. In March 1930, under the new name of United Aircraft and Transport, it merged with Pratt & Whitney, Sikorsky, and Chance Vought. In 1931, with Johnson as president, the airline components, including Boeing Air Transport,

The X-P936, forerunner of the P-26 (*Boeing 5253B*)

were reorganized under the umbrella name of United Air Lines, and Johnson moved his office to Chicago.

Ed had written home during the summer of 1930 that "the total number of employees at Boeing is somewhere in the neighborhood of 200 to 500, varying up and down because if the company gets a project it goes up and if they don't get a contract it goes down. But the Engineering Department has only 50 engineers if you count everybody: engineers, clerical, the works." In 1931 the Engineering Department had expanded to about eighty or ninety people, again counting "the works."

The former Duwamish River shipyard building where Boeing began its business was still in use, but by then the original part had become known as "the shop." The engineering office was in the new administration building, a brick structure, and the whole complex was later known as Plant 1.

Ed's first boss in the summer of 1930 had been Lyle Pierce, of whom Ed said, "He gave me a good education on how to be an apprentice engineer. I started out as an apprentice with all sorts of drafting tasks, but was later able to go into somewhat more complicated engineering activities." In 1931 C. N. Monteith, or "Monty," as everyone called him, was chief engineer and Claire Egtvedt had moved up from chief engineer to the presidency. Now Ed began work for John Ball of the Structures Department. The task—which

The model P-12E (*Boeing 4852B*)

involved very advanced mathematics—concerned the physics of landings on an aircraft carrier deck, with particular emphasis on the problems of the landing gear. These planes were of the F4B series, Navy biplane fighters with single engines. The computations were to determine where to put the hook on the airplane so that when the plane landed, it wouldn't tip over onto its nose and damage the propeller and engine on the flight deck.

After several assignments in the Structures Department, Ed was asked to work on design for the XP-936, a fast pursuit fighter for the Army Air Corps. This wire-braced monoplane with all-metal fuselage became the P-26, the Air Corps' first monoplane pursuit plane. On this plane Ed started out as a group engineer in charge of the flight control system; later he was given the added responsibility for the landing gear.

This was a pretty heavy responsibility for a twenty-year-old, but on August 26, 1931, he turned the magic twenty-one. The birthday letter from his father that year was full of pride and hope:

My dear son:
Tomorrow you will be twenty-one!
I have had many honors since then, but nothing that has happened before or since has had quite the thrill of being your father.

It was not just a passing thrill, for all through the years there has been the joy in our companionship, unutterable pride in your development, and, withal, anxiety for your safety, amounting to anguish when you seemed to be in danger. I don't know how I could have endured it if anything had happened to you. . . .

. . . It would not be possible for me to express in words my ideal of the kind of man you should be. Doubtless you would find it quite difficult to give expression to your own best ideals, but I am sure you have an ideal for yourself, none the less real because of your inability to define it. It is this ideal of your own toward which you must aspire, and not one of my creation for you.

It seems to me that as an engineer the need for such an ideal should be clearly apparent. If an airplane, which is to fly for a few hundred hours and then be scrapped, has to be built according to a carefully drawn plan, certainly a life, which is to go on forever, should be built by a plan no less carefully drawn. Such a plan should be something more than theory; into it should go the wisdom of all that have built before.

There is great need for such a man as you may become. Your profession will lead you to give emphasis to the development and use of material forces, but it is my prayer that you may also make some real contribution to the development and use of those spiritual forces, which alone can bring the world out of its present chaos. . . .

Sometime during that year, Ed became a design engineer for the P-12E. The Army biplane was, with the exception of a few details, the same as the Navy F4B-4. On his own, Ed made a model of the P-12 with about a twenty-five-inch wingspan, probably fashioned in his landlady's basement. The model moved along with Ed's family for about fifty years and eventually was donated to the Boeing Company for display.

During the winter of 1931–32, also in his landlady's basement, Ed managed to assemble enough suitable lumber to build a boat—although not a very big one. Lake Washington was out there in all its vast beauty, and boating, seemingly, was the thing to do if you lived in Seattle. By spring the boat was finished and Ed was able to buy a used outboard motor to power the craft for transportation upon the lake and a used Ford coupe for transportation on the road. In the April 1934 issue of *The Boeing News*, the "Personal Notes" column twitted Wells and an engineer friend concerning the small size of their handmade boats: "E.C. Wells and R.H. McElroy are devoting all their spare time to marine construction, so don't be surprised if you see them cruising around in palatial yachts this summer."

Many of the people who came to Boeing at approximately the same time as Ed remained there in important posts throughout

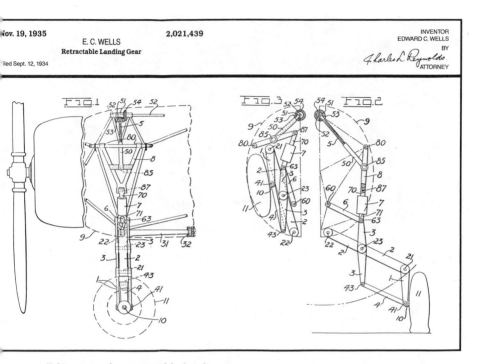

Nov. 19, 1935   2,021,439

E. C. WELLS

Retractable Landing Gear

Filed Sept. 12, 1934

INVENTOR
EDWARD C. WELLS
BY
Charles L. Reynolds
ATTORNEY

Ed's patent for retractable landing gear

their working years. They formed an elite cadre for the company, and their families remained Ed's close lifelong friends. These men included George Martin, George Snyder, Harold Adams, and Richard Stith, all recent college graduates. Martin was assigned to what he calls the "cigar-nosed Navy plane."

A. I. Ostlund, whose middle name was Isadore, began to play golf with Ed in the spring of 1932. The young engineer preferred to be known as Izzy. One day he invited Ed to go home with him to meet his family at Bryn Mawr, a small community nestled along the southwest shore of Lake Washington. Izzy's parents were people of proud Scandinavian ancestry. In that home Ed met Izzy's sister, Dorothy Evangeline, and fell in love. From that day he dated her exclusively.

Ed's next assignment at Boeing in 1933 was work on the 247 twin-engined transport, where he impressed his supervisors with his detail drawings on the empennage. The predecessor of the 247 was the unorthodox B-9, a 1931 plane that Ed remembered as "a

Dorothy and Ed

forerunner of the sleek, all-metal bombers which were to follow." It was nicknamed the "Panatela" because of its snub-nosed, slender, cigar-shaped fuselage. The commercial 247, which came in 1933, was the first modern air transport, opening the way for larger and more sophisticated propeller-driven commercial airplanes.

The 247 and the B-9 illustrated Boeing's successful conversion from the wood-wire-fabric–covered plane, through the part-wood, part-metal plane such as the Model 40, to the all-metal structure-and-skin plane. Ed recalled the change-over in his interview with Donald Schmechel:

> We had just gone through the transition from the old stick-and-wire days to the all-metal monoplane with retractable landing gear. It was quite a transition for anyone to make. I think perhaps two things happened to make it desirable to change from wood to all-metal planes. With wood you have to have premium grade lumber and it got harder to come by. The best of lumber is not uniform and you have to allow for structural variations. Metal is much more uniformly reliable. This drove you in the direction of all-metal construction, including a metal skin. What you might call a composite airplane used biplane wings made out of wood with fabric coverings. The next step in the transition was the development of the monocoque fuselage structure with a smooth skin and wood biplane wings; and after that one goes to an all-metal wing and fuselage with the smooth exterior wing of the P-26.

Ed himself faced a potential crisis in his life at the end of his first year at Boeing. He had been so deeply immersed in his work at the plant and his romance with Dorothy that he had forgotten he had applied for a spot in the on-the-job training program in design at the Chrysler Corporation in Detroit. At that time they had advised all applicants that their program would take no more candidates until further notice.

The delayed offer from Chrysler came during the summer of 1932. They had reestablished the on-the-job training program in automobile design and had, as Ed put it, "sweetened the salary offer considerably." The first summer at Boeing, Ed had been paid $115 per month, increased to $125 per month in 1931–32. Chrysler offered considerably more, and Ed decided to accept:

> It sounded so attractive. I sent in the quick reply requested and resigned my job at Boeing. I was ready to take on Detroit, but I still had a date with Dorothy that evening, when I thought I would be saying good-bye. But it didn't turn out that way. During a restless night, for the first time I saw and read the "hand-writing on the wall." It said, "You jerk! Your destiny

is in aviation. This is my final warning! Signed, Lady Luck." So, very
early the next morning I got to the plant and asked Boeing if I could have
my job back. I wired Chrysler to apologize for leading them on, and
called Dorothy to tell her I wouldn't be leaving after all. I must say, she
didn't seem to be the least bit surprised.*

After this the romance became serious, but every time Ed proposed marriage, Dorothy would patiently explain to him that she
had no intention of getting married until she finished college. She
had completed a year at the University of Washington and joined a
sorority whose sisters she had come to cherish. Years later she
said, "No girl ever got more proposals from the same man. Every
time we dated, Ed ended the evening with another proposal, promising me that, if I would marry him, he would see to it that I got that
diploma." Dorothy had dropped out of college and gone to work as
a legal secretary to help pay for a brother's education. Finally, Ed
prevailed, and a date for the wedding was set for the summer of
1934, near their mutual birthday of August 26.

The year 1934 became famous in aviation circles as the year of
"the big bust-up," when a senatorial investigation into Ocean and
Airmail Contracts got under way. Hugo L. Black, at that time Senator from Alabama, persuaded President Franklin Roosevelt that in
1930 Postmaster General Walter Fogler Brown had called the airline
executives to a meeting in his office to discuss the airmail contract
bidding "in an atmosphere of fraud and collusion." Phil Johnson of
Boeing (and United Air Lines) had been, of course, present at that
meeting. At the conclusion of the senate investigation, the Roosevelt administration canceled all airmail contracts, turned the airmail over to the Army Air Corps, and decreed that all executives
who attended Brown's meeting be blacklisted and banned from any
contact with the air transport industry for a period of five years.
The government also demanded the breaking up of the companies,
insisting that there be no corporate connection between airlines
and companies that were building airplanes. United was cut up
into three corporate pieces—East and West Coast manufacturing
being cut off from transport. Boeing's share of United Aircraft and
Transport amounted to $582,000, a frighteningly small amount with
which to maintain a Seattle crew of 712 persons of whom 153 were

*From Ed Wells' acceptance speech on receiving the Tony Jannus Award for 1985.
Text in author's files.

Jack Kylstra (*Boeing 7236B*)   Claire Egtvedt (*Boeing 2926B*)

engineers. Bill Boeing sold out in disgust and Clair Egtvedt became Boeing president.

As a sad footnote to the affair, when the mails were carried by the Army Air Corps, eleven lieutenants and one private crashed their planes in inclememnt weather and were killed in a period of six weeks, at which time airmail carrying was transferred back into commercial hands.

Now Ed Wells comes back into the picture.

Boeing was able to use what it learned from construction of mail-planes such as the Model 200 Monomail to make the 247 the first modern airliner. And in June 1934 Boeing was awarded a design contract by the Army Air Corps for a plane that would test the limits of aircraft engineering.

At the time of his marriage Ed was continuing work on the 247 and also working under Jack Kylstra on the new contract, dubbed Project A, later to be known as the XB-15. This enormous four-engined bomber has sometimes been confused with the later project, called by the trademark name of "Flying Fortress," officially listed as the B-17.

The giant XB-15 was the largest plane built at that time in the

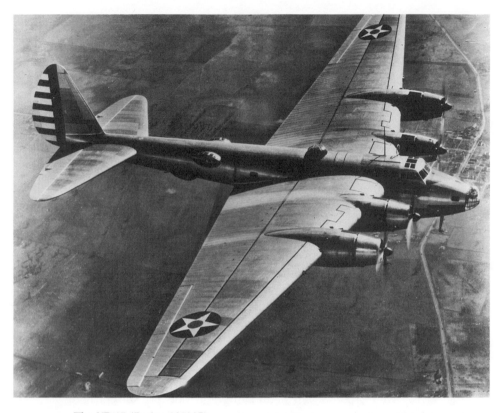

The XB-15 (*Boeing 10520B*)

United States. A spoof of the project appeared in the October 1937 issue of the *Air Corps Newsletter,* and the humor may hold some clues as to why the Air Corps decided on a smaller plane.

> Because of the distance between the motors, the most practical means of communication is the radio. A constant check on the weather is necessary. The fact that the crew on one engine might be enjoying perfect weather while the crew on the neighboring engine might be engulfed in a blizzard, makes the weather report all important. Each member of the crew on this super plane is equipped with a compass and ten days' emergency rations, provided in case he should become lost going to work. The average citizen isn't allowed to go aboard this craft to inspect, due to the fact that the last one who got aboard unnoticed, wasn't found for days.

Only one prototype XB-15 was ever built. Although the plane set several load-to-altitude records, and in fact was used as a cargo transport until it was scrapped in 1945, it was too underpowered to be successful as a bomber. "The lag in power plant development," writes aviation historian Jay Spenser, "was a constant frustration to airframe manufacturers of that era."*

The idea for the airplane which did become the famous Flying Fortress, and which brought Ed so much attention, was conceived by Claire Egtvedt sometime after his visit in 1928 to San Diego to witness a demonstration of aircraft carriers and Navy fighter planes of Boeing manufacture. Egtvedt set up a conference with Admiral Joseph M. Reeves, who did not think much, apparently, of air defense in its current state as compared with his own Navy guns, although he did concede that Boeing fighters could help to keep enemy planes from reaching his battleships.

The story has been told by many reporters, even by Bill Barnes in *America's Air Ace Comics:* Egtvedt suggests to the admiral that a fleet of Boeing fighters carrying enough bombs could be a powerful striking force. Reeves compares the puny firepower of the fighters to the (according to the admiral's figures) 100 million foot-tons of destructive force from one battleship. "The airplane just isn't a dreadnaught!" scoffs the admiral. In the comic book, Egtvedt says, "We're going to build an air battleship."

Egtvedt remembered vividly the scene he witnessed in 1923 when the controversial "Billy" Mitchell led bombing runs on the surplus battleships *Virginia* and *New Jersey*. It had taken a lot of bombs and several runs at varying altitudes, but the great ships had gone under.

In recalling his start on the B-17 bomber, Ed told Donald Schmechel, "After I decided to stay with Boeing, the job and every-thing else in my life took a turn for the better, and I now had a clear professional goal ahead. After doing several structural and system design jobs on airplanes such as the F4B Navy fighters, the P-12 se-ries for the Air Corps, the P-26 Air Corps pursuit and the 247 trans-port, I had the good fortune to be assigned to do the preliminary work on a series of possible bomber designs for the Air Corps, with the opportunity thus to participate in an aviation turning point."

On August 6, 1934, the Army Air Corps sent out requests for

*Jay Spenser, letter to the author, April 6, 1989.

bids on a flying prototype for a new "multi-engined" bombardment airplane. The prototype was to be delivered by August 1935. Boeing engineers debated what the "multi-engined" description meant to the Air Corps. They eventually suggested that a four-engined plane should be the way to go, since the competing firms—Martin and Douglas—would most likely bid on their two-engined designs. Egtvedt made a rush trip to Wright Field to ask, very quietly, if a four-engined plane would be considered. The answer from the Air Corps officer was something like this: "The proposal says multi-engined, doesn't it?"

Ed always credited Claire Egtvedt with the genesis of the B-17 idea. He told the Portland *Oregonian* for January 24, 1943, that Egtvedt had "the vision to interpret 'multi-engine' to mean 'four-engine' and then to persuade the Boeing Board of Directors to authorize the construction of the prototype for the B-17, although its cost would exceed the total financial resources of the company. Without his foresight and his courage, we might have entered World War II with the small Douglas two-engined B-18 instead of the mighty four-engined B-17."

Specifications for the plane were these: bomb load, 1 ton; range, 1,020 miles; speed, 200 to 250 miles per hour; crew, 4 to 6. Because it would be larger, speedier, greater in range, and steadier than any bomber built before, Egtvedt was certain it would be his "dreadnaught of the skies."

Since the announcement of the competition was received on August 8, and the completed plane would have to be delivered one year from that date, the engineering staff began to work with a frenzy. "Giff" Emery was named project manager and Ed Wells, not yet having reached his twenty-fourth birthday, was named his assistant. It would be around-the-clock to get the work done.

Ed was scheduled to marry Dorothy Ostlund in the Bryn Mawr Methodist Church on August 25. The invitations had gone into the mail and the wedding presents had begun to arrive. Boeing, as a great concession, promised Ed two days for his honeymoon (Sunday and Monday). Dorothy and Ed decided on a quick trip to Vancouver, British Columbia.

The wedding was a beautiful affair. Dorothy wore a veil crowned and bordered by Princess Point lace, handmade by Ed's mother and previously used by Ed's sisters at their own weddings. Ed's younger sister Peggy was one of the bridesmaids.

For their first home, Ed and Dorothy rented a semifurnished apartment at the Fairfax, on Capitol Hill near St. Mark's Cathedral.

Artist's rendering of Ed at twenty-four as he designed the B-17 Flying Fortress in the Red Barn (Warren McCallister, artist)

After the ceremony Ed had to beg blankets from one of his sisters for their first night together. Life had been so hectic that he and Dorothy had not had time to shop.

Of course, one of their wedding gifts had come in the form of a letter of advice from Ed's father:

> I suppose that this will be my last letter to you before the big event. With this in mind, I am not going to do much preaching on this occasion,

Dorothy and Ed, August 1934

much as I might feel like it. You are wise enough to know that the step you are taking is a momentous one, and that life from now on will never be quite the same. It can be very much richer and fuller than it has ever been before, and my prayer is that it may be so. On the other hand it can be poorer and more restricted. A happy married life does not just happen; there are so many things that can spoil it. Love itself is not altogether involuntary, neither is it altogether biological. Love can be controlled and directed as to its object and can be deeply spiritualized in character. Because love is of deep spiritual significance, my hope and prayer is that you and Dorothy, in laying the foundation for your life together, may build into those foundations the pattern of a profound faith in God and a real sense of His guidance in all the matters that come up. . . .

You and Dorothy will have special problems of your own, if Dorothy continues to work. These in particular will have to be met in a spirit of helpfulness and understanding. I guess no man likes to do housework; perhaps women don't like it either, but it has to be done, and the woman can't do it all and work in an office too.

You know, I think, that we love Dorothy and have taken her into our hearts as a daughter, and a real member of the clan. If you use as good taste and judgment in other things as you have in choosing a wife, you will get on fine. . . .

Limited as they were by time for the honeymoon, Ed and Dorothy were more acutely limited by funds. Ed was making $125 per month and Dorothy was being paid $90 as a legal secretary. Dorothy confessed later that they returned from Vancouver with only five dollars to live on until the next paychecks arrived.

Ed told *Aero Digest* in February 1951 that "after that two-day honeymoon my bride didn't see much of me for a month—it was more exactly three weeks—in those three weeks the prototype Fortress acquired the basic form it carried throughout the war." Of course, it was not the "Fortress" when it began. It was not even the B-17 (the Army designation), since the Air Corps had only asked for a design and prototype to be "looked at" one year from that August. It would have to be a company-financed plane, and the Depression along with "the big bust-up" had left the company with very little cash. The only days that could be cut off the 365-day deadline would be in engineering.

A glass partition was put up to wall off a small space in which Ed worked with his helpers. Signs appeared on that glass saying, "Restricted Access," and the War Department backed them up with warnings of fines and prison sentences for revealing secrets of "the mystery ship's" progress. Boeing dubbed the plans Project 299 and refused to discuss it with the press. Years later, Ed recalled those high-pressure weeks:

We were up against a deadline of an army competition. A plane had to be conceived, designed, wind tunnel tested, built and flight-tested—all in less than 12 months! There didn't seem any way to cut down the construction time, so it was up to us engineers to reduce our designing time to as near nothing as possible. . . .

During three weeks the Fortress acquired the basic shape it still has today.

We designed it to carry all bombs internally, principally to cut down air resistance.

We determined to install more guns than in use then, and to fire from enclosures. We believed that this was the first bomber to have guns in turrets.

We agreed on constant speed propellers. They added weight and cost, but we computed they would more than pay out on a bomber.

We figured the pilots and crew were entitled to the comfort and protection of a sound-proofed and heated cabin. Bombers then in use had single-seat cockpits and sliding canopies.

We developed control tabs on the trailing edges of rudder and elevators. These "bit" into the air first and pulled the larger control surfaces with them. This made a large plane easily controllable.

We eliminated every obstruction to airflow that we could. We kept the external surface as smooth as possible. The standard bomber surface of the time had some corrugated metal externally.

Once the large picture was outlined, all the details to carry out construction had to be drawn and blueprinted. This was the day of the slide rule, the inking pen, the draftsman's compass, the adding machine—no photocopy, no solar-powered calculator, no computer graphics with printout (an engineer might say "no CAD, no CAM"). A B-17 took a draftsman's drawing for every one of its 65,000 separate parts, and there were also those quarter million rivets, tens of thousands of spot welds, and thousands of nuts and bolts. If spread out on the ground, the blueprints for a B-17 would have covered 150 acres. With the rush to get into production, the engineers had been unable to do preliminary wind tunnel testing until *after* the blue-printing. But the engineering work had been done with such precision that when the tests were completed, the results did not require a single major revision.

In December Ed was promoted to Acting Project Engineer on the 299, and work for everybody had begun to be almost around-the-clock. By late spring some of the men were working double shifts and taking naps in their cars.

Ed wrote to his father on June 29, 1935, after the plane had gone on public view and he was free to discuss it:

The Boeing Model 299, prototype of the B-17 (*Boeing 8184B-10*)

It's almost nine o'clock and I'm just getting home from work. That is the regular thing now, so you can guess that we're in the midst of preparing the ship for flight, at last. Had the plane completely assembled yesterday for the first time, and wheeled it out on the apron for the first motor run. Discovered a few bugs in the fuel system which have kept us busy all day fixing, getting ready for the taxi and brake tests. Probably the first flight will be staged Friday.

The day before this letter was written, the Seattle newspapers had gone wild with praise and speculation as the separate parts of Project 299 (the fuselage and the two wings) were rolled out of the plant. (The gun turrets were kept under wraps.) At that time there were few buildings large enough to shelter such a giant, and the parts had to be brought for final joining out on the tarmac at the edge of Boeing Field. A shortened version of the *Seattle Star*'s article is quoted here:

Assembling of what is purported to be the world's fastest superbomber was begun today at Boeing Company's hangar at Boeing Field. Under construction secretly at the Boeing plant for the past year, the "mystery plane" was moved piecemeal from the factory to the field today. Persons who saw the various parts being moved thru the streets, declared it appears to be of unusual size. Under War Department regulations The Boeing Company has kept a cloak of secrecy over the progress of the plane's construction and it is only because it was necessary to move its parts thru the streets that word of the mystery has reached the public.

It will carry an unusually heavy load of bombs and it is plain that it could be equipped with a number of machine guns.

It is rumored that test flights, to be conducted later this month, will reveal that it is the fastest craft of its kind in the world. Rumors declare it will make between 250 and 300 miles per hour. Radically new aeronautical theories appear to have been incorporated.

One wing of the giant craft left the plant for the field at 6 A.M. It appears to be between 50 and 65 feet long. The fuselage was taken over shortly after noon and the other wing was to go over late in the day. A crowd of the curious watched the piecemeal moving of the huge bomber.

Boeing officials refused to give out any details about the plane.

Ed sent his father copies of a single picture in the *Seattle Times* and three much larger stretched-out pictures from the *Seattle Star*. The *Star* had lettered across the wing span an estimate of 105 feet; the actual span turned out to be 103 feet, 9 inches. Ed hand-lettered across his copies arrows indicating where he was standing, and comments including: "me still working"; "the co-designer, better known as your boy"; "again—quite proud of my baby" and with one picture in which he does not appear with the plane, "the only one I didn't spoil."

Dick Williams, a reporter for the *Seattle Times*, inadvertently bestowed upon the superbomber its immortal name of "Flying Fortress" on that date. Headlining a photograph of the plane taken head-on, he titled the picture "15-TON FLYING FORTRESS" and his story under the picture reads: "Declared to be the largest land plane ever to be built in America, this fifteen-ton flying fortress built for The Boeing Airplane Company under Army specifications, today was ready to test its wings."

What a fortunate name, having in it a lilt of music, a touch of romance, a boast of pride, and a sound people found they loved to roll off their tongues. What if it had been christened "The Flying Dreadnaught"? Or "The Soaring Battleship"? Or something similar to "The Spruce Goose"? The Boeing Company was charmed with

Les Tower (*Boeing 4051B*)

the newspaper caption and applied for a copyright on the name—
so Flying Fortress it has been for over fifty years.

National newspapers began to print banner headlines concerning the roll-out of the plane for its test flights, and even the famous
columnist Ed Sullivan was intrigued. With his usual overdramati-
zation he wrote in his syndicated column "Little Old New York":

> On June 28, 1935, the Model 299 rolled out on the Boeing Field in Seattle,
> Washington. As the sun glinted on the huge four-engined job, one wom-
> an trembled with pride: she was Mrs. Edward Wells, bride of the 24-
> year-old boy who designed what will make history as the Flying For-
> tress; Boeing's Claire Egtvedt's emotions were mixed: he had persuaded
> his company, in this depression year, to put all its eggs in one basket
> and Model 299 is the basket and bombs are the eggs.

The actual test flights were most prosaic, although there were
crowds around Boeing Field and excited viewers all over Seattle
watching every time the plane went into the air. All flight-testing
was done with Les Tower, Boeing's colorful test pilot, at the controls. Tower was a native of Polson, Montana (also Dorothy Wells's

birthplace). He was a former cowboy who had decided he'd rather ride saddle in the cockpit, so enlisted in the Army Air Corps and took training at Langley Field in Virginia. After receiving an engineering degree from the University of Washington, he started flying Boeing planes in 1925. The company felt that "299" could not be in better hands.

In a speech to the Seattle Chapter of the American Institute of Aeronautics and Astronautics in 1974, Ed described the Seattle testing:

> The airplane was rolled out of the Boeing Field hangar on July 17, 1935, and after a few hitches during taxi tests, including the problem of the tail shimmy, the first flight took place on July 28, with Les Tower as pilot, Louis Wait as co-pilot and Henry Igo of Pratt and Whitney as flight engineer. Due to the lack of time and possibly lack of funds, this was a very limited flight test program—seven flights, 14 hours, 15 minutes in all, in a period of three weeks.

The Boeing team had completed the giant plane eleven months after getting the Army specifications, one month ahead of schedule. Peter Bowers, a respected freelance writer and Boeing engineer, researched the vital statistics of the 299 project and computed the workers' wages at an average of 74 cents per hour. Ed said that his own pay came to about 65 cents per hour, and if unpaid overtime had been included he had worked for 50 cents an hour. In spite of the pay, Ed said, "the productivity was relatively good, as interest in the new project was high, and everyone knew how much was at stake on the project. Even the security on the project was good, as the first publicity appeared when pictures were taken of the wings and fuselage on the way to the Boeing hangar for final assembly."

The time had come to deliver the plane at Dayton, Ohio. Ed was chosen to go with Claire Egtvedt to Wright Field for the fly-off competition. "This was quite an assignment for me," Wells recalled fifty years later. "At that time I was only 24 years old, and this was to be my first trip ever as a representative of the company. I will always be grateful to Claire Egtvedt, first because he had enough confidence in me to pick me for the job, and second because he was always available for counsel and help whenever I really needed it."*

*From speech made by Ed Wells in July 1985, on the occasion of the fiftieth anniversary of the Boeing Model 299.

The B-17B (*Boeing 11754B*)

Shortly before the trip he wrote again to his father:

> The very idea almost scares me stiff, but I'll do my best to justify the faith the company is putting in me. It seems as though the jobs are getting bigger even faster than I could possibly imagine, so I only hope that I can keep even with them as they come. This is the biggest responsibility I've ever had, making some of the things I've been proud of before seem easy by comparison.
>
> It's as you once told me, too, that up the ladder one has to deal more with men than things. I've had my fling at the task of creating and developing ideas and have gained a measure of confidence in my ability to see through engineering problems, of which we've certainly had our share on the project. Now I'm to have a chance to match my personality and ingenuity with the competition. How I'll measure up remains to be seen.

Ed's flight to Dayton was not a very fast trip. Flying commercial in those days sometimes was just about as fast as going by train. His report of the trip, in a letter to his parents dated August 16, 1935, underscores the leap that aviation took with the B-17.

After a trip that alternated long stretches of glassy smooth weather and short stretches of quite rough air, we're settled in Dayton. Saw the folks in Boise for a minute or two. One motor quit practically cold between Boise and Salt Lake, almost necessitating a forced landing and making us late at Salt Lake. Head winds from Salt Lake doubled the number of stops, and consequently the quantity of rough air to be flown through the descending and climbing each time to the smooth air at about 8 to 10,000 feet. We stopped at the Palmer House for Thursday afternoon and evening in Chicago, having dinner there with Mr. Collier and Mr. West, United Airline officials. We came on to Dayton on the Pennsylvania Railroad last night. Went out to Wright Field today, getting acquainted with a good many of the men here.

Dayton seems a very pleasant place, though the weather is decidedly cooler than average. Had a hard rainstorm this noon to remind us the coast is not the only wet place on the map. Apparently there has been more than the average rainfall this summer, too, for the whole country is quite green, and the Miami is yet a river.

Real work hasn't started yet, awaiting the arrival of the ship, so I have a little time to wish I could be back home again, but at the same time, I'm anxious to get going at the job again as soon as the airplane puts in its appearance. More of news later as it happens.

On the morning of August 20 at Boeing Field, Les Tower took up his position in the pilot's seat of the first Flying Fortress. Louis Wait was in the copilot's position, with Henry Igo aboard as engine monitor and C. W. (Bud) Benton as mechanic. The plan was to fly the plane to Dayton nonstop if possible, with one stop at Cheyenne, if necessary. All was carefully checked out and the plane took off, as one reporter put it, "like a veteran of the air.'" At 3:45 that morning they headed east. Harold Mansfield records in *Vision* that Igo came into the cockpit two hours after liftoff, announced the engines were all doing fine, and said, "Let's give it the works."

After nine hours, three minutes, Tower brought the plane down on the runway at Wright Field, Dayton, breaking all world records: 2,100 miles, nonstop, at an average speed of 232 miles per hour, using only 63 percent power from the engines. Their altitude had averaged out at 12,500 feet, with part of the trip on automatic pilot.

Tower, Wait, Igo, and Benton had anticipated a crowd to greet this outstanding feat of engineering prowess. Only Ed Wells and Claire Egtvedt stood on the field to welcome them. Benton said, "Where's everybody?" To which Ed laughed and replied, "You're not supposed to be here yet. The folks here at Wright don't expect you for another three hours."

Ed was pleased, although he had lost a bet. "While the flight was under way, a pool was put together to estimate the time of flight," he said. "Claire and I evidenced our conservative nature by losing on the high side. Hugh Gosselin of Pratt and Whitney Engines won the bet with the only really close estimate."

Soon the Army tests started in earnest. Leonard Harman (always called Jake) was the bombardment project officer at the base. Years later Ed learned that their parents had been friends in Boise and that he and Jake had attended Sunday School together as small boys. Lieutenant Harman would be in charge of the tests.

These tests proved to be extremely rigorous and the strain was heavy on everyone. In his speech to the American Institute of Aeronautics and Astronautics, Ed described some of the problems they encountered:

> As is usually the case, technical and shop support of the single prototype airplane, with a very limited spare parts availability, turned out to be a more than full time job for our limited support team. . . .
>
> The most difficult situation that I recall was that which followed an engine failure in one of the early tests, requiring a complete engine change. The tight test schedule required the change to be made in a minimum of elapsed time, if we were not to fall behind in competitive tests. There was no time to get reinforcements from Seattle, let alone funds to finance their travel to Dayton and return.
>
> Henry Igo of Pratt and Whitney found a replacement P and W Hornet engine on one of the test stands at the Wright Field power plant laboratory, and we were able to borrow a crane and a makeshift weather shelter from Wright Field sources. Everyone fell to, and beginning the job during the afternoon, working around the clock, we were able to complete the ground check the next morning, followed by a flight test checkout, in time to resume the competitive flight tests on schedule in the afternoon.
>
> Tests went well, and although the high speed performance was not as good as we had estimated, overall performance was excellent in comparison to two other entries—the Douglas, a DC-2/DC-3 derivative, and the Martin, a derivative of the B-10.

Ed had one of the thrills of his life during these weeks at Wright Field. He was told that Orville Wright was on the field and would like to have a tour of the Fortress. Forty-five years later Ed recalled the incident vividly: "As I showed him through the airplane, he made a lasting impression on me, saying, even as he marveled at the new design, that it seemed a pity that aeronautical development seemed to require an undue proportion of effort devoted to military aircraft."*

*From speech by Ed Wells at the 1980 Aerospace Congress and Exposition banquet, October 15, 1980.

The tests had almost come to an end by the week of Halloween. There was only one more to go. The Fortress had outclassed its rivals in every category, including endurance, speed, service ceiling, structure and design, engines and power plant systems, armament and equipment, maintenance, utility as a type, and landing characteristics. Major Ployer Hill, chief of Wright Field's Testing Section and a native of Yakima, Washington, was assigned the position of test pilot on this last evaluation. Major Donald Putt was to be copilot. Les Tower would go along as Boeing observer.

The night before this final test Ed had written to his parents:

> We have been more than making up for our inactivity of the first weeks here, and have put in some long hours out in the worst weather, keeping the airplane in trim for the tests by the Air Corps. It is a wonder that we are not all down with pneumonia, but guess that we are getting to be quite tough now.
>
> It looks as though we might still be here at the first of the year, since the evaluation board is to have their first meeting at the field next Monday and they intend to test the three airplanes quite thoroughly before one is decided on. They will have until December 22nd to place the order, so we should know what the verdict is by that time at least, then there will probably be some time spent after that before I can go home.

On October 30 the world came tumbling in. The plane went into the air for that final test as Ed stood on the ground watching. For a few seconds all looked right, then the plane suddenly started into a steep ascent, straight up at an angle that no plane could maintain. At a height of about 200 feet it fell off on one wing into a dive straight for the ground.

Ed knew exactly what had happened, but no scream from him could have reached the plane. Major Hill had forgotten to check out "all systems go" before he started the flight. In getting into his seat, he had stepped across the locking mechanics that controlled the rudder and the ailerons and had failed to unlock these controls.

As the plane hit the ground it burst into flames. Jake Harman commandeered a truck on the field and rushed to attempt a rescue at the risk of his own life. Putting a coat over his head, he managed to pull Les Tower and Ployer Hill from the burning plane. Don Putt had managed to jump out the front of the wreckage and was gashed and burned. Two other crewmen escaped from the back of the plane. Tower and Hill were rushed to the hospital, where Hill died that afternoon. Tower was badly burned, but there seemed to be some hope of his survival. And Ed was devastated. He told me afterwards that "it was just as if, when the plane crashed, I had seen a child of mine slain in front of my eyes and I could do nothing to save it."

Among Ed's papers was found the original telegram which informed Boeing in Seattle of the tragedy. It reads:

POSTAL TELEGRAPH   WRIGHT FIELD OHIO
Mr. Minshall
Boeing Aircraft Co Seattle Wash
Your bomber just cracked up and caught fire
Still burning
Sgt Price telegraph operator

That night Ed added a postscript to his letter to his parents: "As you have now learned from the papers, the '299' crashed and burned this morning. Our plans are thus all up in the air, but will write as soon as we get down to earth again."

4

The Fortress Rises from the Ashes and Goes to War

A telephone call was put in to Claire Egtvedt at the Palmer House in Chicago, where he was earnestly negotiating with United Air Lines for the sale of some Boeing transport planes. The 299 project had cost over $600,000 for the one plane, and the company was as a consequence on the verge of bankruptcy. Someone had to tell Egtvedt that his $600,000 was now nothing but a heap of smoldering ashes on the runway at Wright Field. Only anguished silence could respond to such tragic news; then Egtvedt managed to say, "I'll be there as quickly as I can make it."

Meanwhile, Wells maintained his characteristic calm. "Anyone not quite as composed as Ed Wells might've come unglued," one coworker told *Aero Digest* in 1951. "Anything he does he does well and quietly," said another friend and fellow engineer. "He's the kind of guy who, if his office caught fire, would most likely call a meeting and discuss what to do about it before taking any action— but he's the kind of guy who would himself put out the fire. Nothing, but nothing, apparently disturbs this calm."

At first it looked as if Les Tower would survive his injuries. Egtvedt and Wells and one of the ranking Air Corps officers at Wright had been able to interview Tower as he lay bandaged in his hospital bed, and they assured him that what had happened was in no way his fault. But Tower insisted he should have noticed that the lock on the controls had not been disengaged. Perhaps with modern burn treatment he might have been saved, but his body could not shake off the toxicity of the burned tissue. Before the week was out he was gone, a man loved by all who knew him and especially admired by Ed. A year later a bronze plaque bearing

Tower's likeness and the inscription "Airman–Friend–Unfailing in Devotion to Duty" was hung in the lobby of Boeing's administration building.

"The loss of life was the greatest loss, as is always the case," Ed told Peter Bowers. "But in addition, the future of the project and of the Company looked pretty dim at this point. . . . I remained at Wright Field to continue discussion and negotiation with the Air Corps, and to await the outcome of the competition. The 299 was clearly the superior airplane."

Egtvedt did what he could to find friends and supporters of the plane in Washington, D.C. Dorothy had come to join Wells in a rented apartment in Dayton some time during September and was a great support during these uncertain times. The waiting for the Army's decision stretched out in what seemed interminable hours and days.

On November 7, Brigadier General A. W. Robbins sent a telegram to the Army Air Corps officials in Washington, which announced that "the recent crash of the Boeing bombing plane beyond doubt was not due to structural failure of the plane." The message further urged Army officials "in the interest of the manufacturer to release immediately this portion of the report."

A wire service news story dated the same day reported that

Wright Field officials said that engine failure was not the cause of the crash which caused one death [Tower was still alive] and injury to four others. . . .

Reports current here and which are given credence by Air Corps officers were that the ailerons of the plane were still locked when the ship took off.

Ailerons are locked on Army fields while planes are "on the line" to prevent swaying.

Col. Frederick L. Martin, commandant of the field, answered these reports by admitting that such a condition might have existed.

That The Boeing Company may not be entirely out of the competition for Air Corps contracts in which the Douglas Aircraft Company, Santa Monica, Calif., and the Glenn L. Martin Company, Baltimore, are also entered, was seen in the announcement that the Bomber Evaluation Board, which has been meeting here to study the merits of the three planes, has suspended its work indefinitely.

. . . Although official confirmation is lacking, it is understood that another plane to take the place of the one which crashed may be built for entrance in the plane competition.

The Boeing bomber had undergone virtually all of the static tests, prior to the crash. The fatal flight was one of the final tests.

Building another $600,000 plane out of company funds was "rabbit out of the hat" imagination of the reporter who filed the story. Boeing did not have the money. The plane was insured, but Harold Bowman, the company treasurer, was finding that there were loopholes in the policy. The insurance company would pay for damage caused by the crash and fire, but not for any usable parts salvaged from the wreck. If no more planes were ordered or if design changes rendered parts obsolete, Boeing would have to absorb the loss.

Then, on November 23 the Associated Press release from Washington, D.C., carried the headline story "Crash Bars Plane Contract," along with a sub-headline "Firm Not Excluded from Future Dealings."

War Department sources said today that The Boeing Airplane Company's four-engined bomber entry had been eliminated from the present Army Air Corps competition for airplane contracts, but that the firm's planes were not excluded from future purchases by the Army.

The bomber crashed on October 30 while being tested in competition at Wright Field, Dayton, Ohio, fatally injuring two fliers.

Egtvedt had found influential supporters for the plane in Washington, D.C., including Generals Hap Arnold and Tooey Spaatz. But there were also fierce and bitter opponents in Congress and in the War Department. Congress was in a mood of almost militant isolationism—"having a big bomber will get us into war." The War Department had convinced itself that "the four-engined giant" was too big for any but a super-pilot to handle, a conviction that took the crash as its proof.

An Associated Press story from Dayton on November 7 carried the news that the Air Corps had recommended the purchase of sixty-five of the new planes, but this recommendation was overridden in the final decision. "Although we had the superior airplane," Ed said later, "eventually we were disqualified for not having completed all the competitive tests, and Douglas with its two-engined bomber was declared the official winner, getting a production order for 133 of their B-18 planes. It was determined, however, that the 299 would merit a service order of thirteen airplanes plus 'one static test airframe.'" Egtvedt brought back the signed contract to Seattle in January 1936.

In the end, 350 of the Douglas B-18s were built. None were ever used by the United States in combat zones during World War II but

were confined to training jobs and searches for German subma-
rines off the U.S. coasts. These "bombers" were so slow they became sitting targets and proved an embarrassment to the Bomber
Evaluation Board, which had compromised in awarding the B-18
the "default win" in the multi-engined competition.

When the final decision was announced, Ed and Dorothy started
back to Seattle just before Christmas 1935. They detoured by way of
Detroit to pick up a new car at the request of Louis Wait, one of
Boeing's test pilots. That drive, even in difficult winter weather,
gave them a chance for the relaxation of a delayed honeymoon. The
intense pressure of Ed's work on the 299 project had provided no
time for a vacation since they were married a year and a half before.

It was good to get home, but it was to be to a new home—a small
apartment on the shore of Lake Washington in a building partly
supported by pilings out over the water. Their view was spectacular, of water and the distant shore, of the snow-capped Cascade
Mountains and Mount Rainier on the days when these were not
shrouded in clouds. Ed wrote to his parents that he hoped to find
time to use his boat "since now we have the lake at our door."

The financial affairs of Boeing remained perilous. Orders for the
United Air Lines transports that Egtvedt had worked so hard to get
did not materialize. "The 13 bomber airplane order helped get the
Company back on its financial feet, but little more than that," Ed
said later. "The net loss, after insurance recovery, on the 299 Project was almost $500,000."*

There was intense deadline pressure for the thirteen B-17s (Air
Corps designation YB-17, later changed to Y1B-17). Boeing did not
have the space in which to put the bombers together, and there was
little money to build that space. There were 755 employees at the
beginning of 1936, and 1,000 by April 1. An expansion of the East
Marginal Way factory was begun, an act of faith that made it possible to assemble nine planes under one roof.

The financial picture improved in July with an order from Pan
American for six Boeing Clippers, a commercial design based on
the XB-15. (The financial improvement was a brief illusion, as the
Clippers subsequently lost money.) By September 30 the assembly
building of the new Plant 2 was completed, so that the fuselage of
the first B-17 could be moved in.

For Ed the picture also brightened that year. He was promoted to
chief of preliminary design.

*Speech before the Seattle chapter of AIAA, October 22, 1974.

The November 1936 issue of the *Boeing News* reported that on
October 19,

> The big doors of the Boeing hangar at Boeing Field rolled open and a
> group of press photographers stood at attention in the overcast, drizzling
> morning. . . . Moving smoothly sideways out the doorway on a miniature
> railway erected for the purpose, the first of the giant Y1B-17 four-engined
> bombers made its premiere in completed form.
>
> A few minutes later workmen denuded the engines of their cowlings
> and removed the slinger de-icers from the propellers, then proceeded
> with first tests of the plane's powerful new 1000 horsepower Wright Se-
> ries G Cyclone engines. When the great 16-ton aerial defense weapon
> was again rolled inside, the doors closed behind it for further work, more
> tests and minute inspection.
>
> Meanwhile, no. 2 plane was taken to the hangar for final assembly.
> Number 3 has been moved to Plant 2, where work began the first week in
> November.

The Wright Cyclones were installed because the Pratt & Whit-
neys of the 299 were judged to be slightly overpowered. In December 1936 the test flights on the B-17 began. The first delivery was
made January 11, with a stopover at Spokane. Plane no. 2 was ready
for flight-testing, and no. 3 was expected to be ready for testing by
the end of January.

A 1937 issue of the *Boeing News* continued the saga:

> The glint of crisp December sunshine on four propellers driven by pow-
> erful Wright "G" Cyclones attracted an admiring crowd to Boeing Field
> December 2 for the long awaited initial test hop of the giant Y1B-17.
>
> At 10:24 o'clock the big plane roared picturesquely skyward in a first
> takeoff that witnesses unanimously described as "beautiful," with Major
> John D. Corkille at the controls. Along with him were Captain Stanley
> Umstead, head of the flight test section at Wright Field; Captain E. R.
> McReynolds, Langley Field; Lieutenant Leonard F. Harman, project engi-
> neer for bombers, Wright Field; Roy Grooms, Wright Field mechanic;
> and the best wishes of every Boeing employee.
>
> Mrs. Corkille sat intently by the radio in the Air Corps Hangar on the
> field. At 11:05 o'clock the huge bomber landed gracefully after a success-
> ful forty-minute cruise.
>
> Two days later, under a heavy sky that threatened rain, the plane again
> soared upward, this time followed by a United Air Lines Boeing 247D
> transport packed to the last seat with press photographers and newsreel
> men. In an hour it was again on the ground. Major Corkille expressed
> cheerily the results of another satisfactory flight.
>
> The third flight was not charmed. Captain Umstead at the controls,
> Captain McReynolds, Lieutenant Harman, Mark Koogler, Wright Field

mechanic and Mike Pavone, Boeing mechanic, cruised for more than an hour, then alighted with the brakes locked. As a result, the plane "nosed up" and crowds flocked to the field to see. Damage proved superficial, however, and it was expected that a week or ten days would see the plane once more ready for flight, and for delivery at Wright Field at Dayton.

It was a "nose-down" not "up" since the nose buried itself in the asphalt, and the story of that test flight is a bit of a gloss. Umstead had been warned that he had brought the plane to too sudden a halt in a taxi run before the flight and had been told by the Boeing man on board that he had better not retract the landing gear until the brakes had cooled off. Umstead did not take the advice and when the landing was made it was with brakes fused and inoperable. Of course Congress and the War Department again raised the issue of "a plane too big for our best pilots to handle." The birthday letter from Ed's father for 1937 said,

A good deal has happened in the world since my 27th birthday. If anybody had told me that I would have a son who, when he was 27 years old, would be designing and building airplanes to cross the continent and the ocean in a few hours, I wouldn't have believed a word of it. We had read fantastic tales of such things, but nobody believed such things would ever really happen.

Ed and Dorothy decided to find a modest house to rent, since an apartment surrounded by the waters of Lake Washington was not an ideal place for a child, and they were expecting their first that September. They found a rental adjacent to the Mount Baker area of Seattle in time for the birth of Laurie Jo, named after her paternal grandmother, Laura Wells, and her maternal grandmother, Josephine Ostlund.

Since General Frank Andrews, by then Commanding General of the General Headquarters Air Force at Langley, had originally been opposed to the B-17, Ed and the Boeing Company took satisfaction in learning what he had to say in his New Year's message of 1938:

The successful service test and the universal acceptance of the B-17 as the prototype of the future basic element of our Army Air Force—the heavy load, long endurance, high speed multi-engined bomber—is one of the outstanding accomplishments of the year 1937 in the GHQ Air Force.

Memories are notoriously short, but reflection will remind us that one short year ago the modern four-engined bomber, exemplified by the B-17 bombardment plane, was under fire. It was thought to be "too much air-

Ed's pencil sketch of Laurie Jo

plane" for Air Corps personnel—unnecessarily large, costly and complex.

During the past year, GHQ Air Force personnel have proved beyond question by thousands of hours in all weather and dropping thousands of bombs at maneuvering and stationary targets, that the four-engined, heavy load, high performance airplane is not only valuable, but necessary if the Air Force is to execute the role that will fall to it in case of war.*

According to a report dated February 1938, the B-17s delivered to the Army Air Corps up to that date had flown 679,000 miles, or an

*Quoted in *Boeing News*, February 1938.

The Stratoliner, the world's first pressurized airliner (*Boeing 12543B*)

equivalent of more than twenty-seven times around the globe, or over 140 full days in the air.

Jake Harman, back in Dayton, was still pounding the drum for more recognition for the B-17. Colonel Oliver Echols suggested that the fourteenth B-17—the one designated as the "extra" to be used for structural testing—be used in a revolutionary experiment to allow flight at extremely high altitudes with added speed and range. This would be done with turbo-superchargers—turbine paddle-wheel arrangements impelled by the plane's hot exhaust gases, which pumped high-pressure air into the engines for higher power at the thin air of 25,000 to 30,000 feet.

Harman estimated that at 25,000 feet, the B-17 with these super-chargers could fly at just under 300 mph, compared with its current top speed of about 250 mph. Echols and Harman approached Egtvedt with the idea and said they would try to get money from the War Department. Ed said he would get information on turbo-superchargers and see if they could be put on the test plane. But he realized that at those altitudes they would have to provide more than just oxygen masks for the flight crew and passengers. He drew a modification of the B-17 fuselage configuration—a cross-section of the body showed a perfect circle, the most efficient design for a pressurized cabin because it allows the pressurized air to exert its force equally in all directions. The idea of the Boeing Stratoliner was born, changing the picture of commercial (as well as military) flight forever.

This Stratoliner concept, using the tail surfaces and wings and turbo-supercharger of the proposed B-17, so interested Pan Am that they offered to underwrite a part of the cost of development and contracted for three of these planes. TWA ordered six and the Air Corps signed a contract for the development of turbo-super-chargers on all B-17s.

Things seemed to be going well, at long last, for Ed Wells and the B-17. Then Harman came out to Seattle to see how the work was progressing on the turbo-superchargers for the bomber. Ed pointed out to him the Stratoliners being built so that the cabins could be pressurized, hoping he could persuade the Air Corps to pressurize the bombers. Harman's reply was, "I've got bad news for Boeing. The War Department has turned down Echols' request for pressurized bombers. In fact, they have allocated no funds for any four-engined bombers for this new fiscal year."*

It should be mentioned here that the order for those first thirteen B-17s had been delivered, the last plane eleven weeks ahead of schedule. When it was delivered, announcement was made of an order for thirty-nine more, and after that another for thirty-nine. Then came Harman's announcement of no more. In 1938 the exhaust-driven turbo-superchargers on the "test" plane were flight-tested, enabling it to be the first production plane capable of operation at and above 35,000 feet.

Speaking of the situation at Boeing in 1938, Ed said "the loss of the contract for development of the turbo-supercharged Y1B-17A was approximately $140,000. This loss and the $650,000 loss from the 299 were written off against the profit on the basic thirteen-plane order, with the remainder amortized as development expense against the B-17B and the B-17C contracts. This kept the company going until orders were received for later B-17 models." In another speech Ed said that "hindsight tells us that the invest-

*Quoted in speech made by Ed Wells in July 1985, on the occasion of the fiftieth anniversary of the Boeing Model 299.

The Y1B-17A used to test turbo-supercharger installation (*Boeing 11233B*)

ment in the 299 was justified, as was the continuing investment in
the turbo-supercharged version of the YB-17, but not everyone was
sure about that at the time."*

The people at GHQ Air Force at Langley decided on a spectacular
public relations demonstration in an effort to sell the idea of the big
bomber to Congress, the War Department, and the nation. Someone suggested sending six of the big planes in a formation flight to
the inauguration ceremony of Roberto Ortiz as President of Argen-
tina on February 17, 1938. International News Service reported,

> Six United States Army bombers, the giant "Flying Fortress" symbol of
> American good-will, stole the show staged for the inauguration. . . .
>   More than 2,000,000 people stared as the huge bombers maneuvered
> over Buenos Aires in the lead of an aerial armada of nearly 300 American-
> built Argentine fighters in combat formation.
>   Etched against the blue sky, the planes gripped the multitude's atten-

*Speech accepting the Tony Jannus Award in 1985.

tion almost throughout the entire inaugural ceremonies. . . . The "Flying Fortress" drew tumultuous cheers of "Long live our friends of North America."

This was not a nonstop flight. The planes did refuel in Peru. But, led by Lieutenant Colonel Robert Olds, it swept the world off its feet. And it did change the opposition to the B-17 into an enthusiastic love affair. Upon his return, Olds told President Roosevelt, Secretary of War Harry Woodring, and Chief of Staff Malin Craig:

> The plane came up to all expectations—undoubtedly the best flying machine ever built. The Army's six Flying Fortresses proved themselves superior for defense purposes to any other plane in the military service. The ships performed perfectly throughout the cruise, much of which was made above the clouds, out of sight of earth and under adverse weather conditions.
>   This flight demonstrated the ability of big bombers to operate on long distance missions where a number of planes can operate as a single unit. To fly as individuals with each plane navigating its own course, was something new in military aviation. The crews used some oxygen at all altitudes above 12,000 feet and at times the ships climbed to 21,000 feet without ill effects.

Olds reported to Boeing that President Roosevelt was "highly enthusiastic over the results of the flight." And Senator Robert Reynolds of North Carolina rose in Congress to praise the flight as "one of the most celebrated ever made by the army aviators of any country," after which he recommended that the Distinguished Flying Cross be awarded to the commanding officer. Senator Lewis B. Schwellenbach of Washington rose for recognition, but Senator Reynolds refused to yield without a bit more bombast: "I was privileged and honored when I had the opportunity to accompany Senator Schwellenbach to the great Boeing plant, the makers and manufacturers of fighting planes, and I surmise that the Senator from Washington has risen for the purpose of bringing to the attention of this honorable body the fact that the planes which made the memorable flight were constructed within the borders of his great and lovely city of Seattle, in the state of Washington."

This same Congress, this same War Department, even this general commanding at Langley had earlier blocked the B-17. After this stunt flight to South America, they were all tossing bouquets and rushing to crown her "Miss America." On July 1, the Army Air Corps placed another order for thirteen Fortresses, bringing the total to thirteen now in service and thirty-nine on order. (In all of this dealing, nobody seemed to be superstitious about the number thirteen on all reorders.) Louis Johnson, Acting Secretary of War, told reporters that "the Flying Fortress is certainly definite proof that America still holds an unchallenged position of leadership in aeronautical design, despite the fact that other nations are spending many times the money available in this country for that purpose."

In this same year Ed received his promotion to chief project engineer in charge of military projects. And in 1939 Boeing advanced him to assistant chief engineer. With this promotion Ed and Dorothy decided to look for a house to buy. They would like to plan for another child, and Ed wanted a house with a basement which would allow him, at long last, to build the model railway system he had dreamed of since he was a small boy. On Cascadia Avenue in the Mount Baker district, which rises over Lake Washington south of what is now the Mercer Island Floating Bridge, they found a large California Monterey style two-story with a good space in the basement. The miniature railway began to take space soon after they moved in.

The people at Wright Field then began to ask for changes in the B-17 and evolution started on the long series of new B-17 models. This demanded Ed's traveling back and forth to Dayton, sometimes for rather extensive stays. Again, commercial air travel was not what it is today. Ed wrote home after one of his trips to Dayton in March 1939:

> I finally arrived here after quite an eventful trip and am well settled at my own Van Cleve "home" [the Van Cleve Hotel] so that it is time for a letter.
>
> The weather was good from Portland to Pendleton, but there was a delay at Pendleton to decide whether to take off for Salt Lake to beat the weather, or to take off for Boise to wait for an improvement at Salt Lake. We then took off for Boise and there we took a taxi downtown for a wait of about an hour while the fog lifted at Salt Lake. We arrived at Salt Lake without incident except that there weren't very many holes in the low ceiling, and waited there for about an hour while conditions improved. Upon arriving at Cheyenne, we were rolled into a hangar to keep the ship warm, while we slept the rest of the night. About nine o'clock in the morning we were rolled out again and took off for Omaha, landing there in a snow storm. Weather was getting worse at Chicago, so after waiting in Omaha all day we finally took the train overnight to Chicago, and I took the day train to Dayton, arriving one day late.
>
> It was quite a trip, but encouraging in one way, in that the airlines appear to be much more cautious and sensible about the weather they fly in

now than they were formerly. Their attitude will be reflected in their safety record.

Another tragedy struck Boeing that same month. Representatives of the Dutch airline KLM came to Seattle to look over the Boeing Stratoliner and insisted that they try the plane in critical tests at maximum angle of yaw and stall. During the flight, in the sideslip tests which the KLM men had insisted upon, the plane went into a spinning dive. It had to pull out of the dive so suddenly the wings and tail surfaces broke away because of the intense loads put upon them. The plane crashed at the base of Mount Rainier near the small town of Alder. Ten people were killed, including KLM's engineer and test pilot; Jack Kylstra, Boeing's chief engineer and designer of the great XB-15; and Ralph Cram, a longtime Boeing aerodynamicist. Ed thus lost two of his most valued friends and co-workers, and he grieved deeply.

The year 1939 brought many new challenges to Boeing. The war had erupted in earnest in Europe. Those whom Germany was threatening were totally unprepared. "Everybody talks planes and more planes," the *Boeing News* reported in June 1941. "Fighters, dive bombers, medium bombers, because Germany, it is reported, has 50,000 planes."

President Roosevelt authorized the expenditure of $500 million as a rearmament program, with $50 million to be allocated to airplane procurement. Many more B-17s would have to be built. Boeing took out a $5.5 million Reconstruction Finance Corporation loan to provide for expansion of the plant and began to look for a real "pro" to head up the vastly burgeoning company responsibility.

Egtvedt and company attorney Bill Allen hoped they could persuade former Boeing president Phil Johnson to come back to head the company once again. His five-year banishment from the American air industry had at last expired. (The United States Court of Claims, after years of investigation, cleared Johnson in 1943, finding that the airmail contracts with Boeing and United Air Lines had after all "been legally secured through open and competitive bidding rather than through collusion or conspiracy.") Johnson did return to become president of Boeing in 1939 and Egtvedt stepped up to be chairman of the board.

After the death of Jack Kylstra, Wellwood Beall became chief engineer, and Ed was promoted to assistant chief engineer. Ed called Beall "a great guy to work for and a great guy to be a friend of."

Beall was equally enthusiastic about Ed:

Wellwood Beall and Ed (*Boeing P1286*)

Put Ed Wells behind a drawing board, or get him into a huddle with other engineers on a tough problem, then you'll see him sparkle! Time and time again I've watched Ed as he has been called into an engineering conference that has been "stuck" by some complicated problem of design. Ed will listen to the whole story. Someone will ask, "Ed, what do you think about it?" His reply will usually be, "I don't know enough about it yet."

No amount of persuasion will make him "give," but after a while, he'll grab a pencil and hunch over the drawing board. Then things start to happen! More than once I've seen other engineers stand back with their mouths open as Ed Wells has swung into action.

Nineteen thirty-nine had been a strenuous, work-packed year for everyone at Boeing, and 1940 would bring no less in stress and toil. Joy did come to the Wells house on Cascadia, however, for on August 21 a son was born. He was named Edward Elliott for his two grandfathers.

Tragic news poured in from all over Europe, and the pressure for aircraft was intense. The *Boeing News* of June 1941 referred to the

Ed with his son, Edward Elliott, in 1945 (Ed in temporary military uniform for a "secret" trip to Guam)

"Plane of the Year": "The horde comes thundering over Poland. The dreaded Stuka! Poland collapses. France goes under. At Dunkirk the fighting R.A.F. planes hold off the light Nazi bombers until the British can cross the Channel for home. Britain cried out for planes. In spite of polite murmurs about Flying Fortresses being 'flying targets' the United States steps up production of the big four-engined bombers."

Just before the fall of France, June 22, 1940, Boeing had received a contract from the French government for production of 240 DB-7B attack bombers under license from Douglas. When France surrendered to the Germans, Great Britain arranged to take over the contract. This order took Boeing out of a critical financial bind.

In July the War Department placed an order for 512 B-17Es with

Boeing built 380 Douglas DB-7B attack bombers (*Boeing 16760B*)

Boeing, and offered more than $20 million for tools, heavy equipment, and plant expansion. George Schairer and Eddie Allen had joined Boeing the previous year. Schairer was an expert on aerodynamics and Allen, who had been a test pilot since World War I, convinced the Boeing crowd that the work of a test pilot should be to sit in while the plane is being designed rather than being called in to see if it will fly. Schairer and Allen got the first Boeing wind tunnel built, relieving Boeing engineers from having to wait their turn at the wind tunnels at Langley, Cal Tech, and the University of Washington to test those precious model planes—some costing around $16,000 apiece. These two men were set up to manage a Department of Testing at Boeing.

Great Britain was pleading for planes. Twenty Flying Fortresses were sent, but they were not well received.

5

Back to the Drawing Board: The Fortress Clobbers Germany

Many of the first experiences of the Flying Fortresses in combat were dismal. The twenty B-17Cs sent to England were altered slightly to meet British standards, but they still reflected their original purpose as a defensive weapon, designed to protect the coast of the United States from naval attack. They employed the Sperry bombsight, which British pilots found difficult to use. They were not heavily armored and their fuel tanks were not self-sealing (or at least not sufficiently self-sealing). Also the planes were under-armed, lacking powered gun turrets and a tail gunner. The records of their first forays in combat were often accounts of missed targets and vulnerability against the onslaught of German fighter planes.

Actually, the B-17C had been sent to Britain with the express understanding that the planes would be used only for training and never in combat. They had been delivered under the Lend-Lease arrangement between the United States and Britain (the bill passed by Congress at Roosevelt's request on March 11, 1941). In its desperate need for airplanes—any planes—Britain disregarded this provision and sent the Fortresses with untrained crews to bomb targets in the western and northern areas of Europe.

Back in Seattle, Eddie Allen and George Schairer were working hard to overcome the problems reported back from the first combat experiences. Allen said, "At those extremely high altitudes we have a hundred things that can go wrong. Propellers won't work. Grease won't work. The fuel system can go wrong." New self-sealing fuel tanks were installed in the B-17D. Fifty-caliber machine guns were used all around, except in the nose. Additional armor was added, and the intercommunication system was improved.

B-17C's awaiting delivery at Boeing Field in 1940 (*Boeing 15204B*)

Ed and his very much expanded engineering staff were busy refining the Fortress and finally got into production on the D and E models. In early September 1941, the first B-17E was rolled out onto the tarmac at Boeing Field. This Fortress had the first famous dorsal fin, and it had powered gun turrets, and the very important addition of a tail gunner. This plane was built to carry the fight to the enemy.

But there was still a serious problem with the British in the use of the Fortresses as late as 1943. General Ira Eaker was responsible for and commander of the planes for the United States in the European theater. He wanted them to fly deep into Germany in order to destroy the capability of the Germans to pursue the war. With enough clobbering of its aircraft factories and munition plants, he thought, Germany would be so crippled that no land invasion forces would be necessary to force her surrender. And he knew that the Fortresses would have to accomplish this with daylight raids. The Fortresses were easy targets on night bombing because the glow from their turbo-superchargers could not be dimmed. And they were finally using the very secret Norden bombsight, which required daylight.

But the British were firmly committed to night bombing. When President Roosevelt went to the Casablanca Conference of the Allied High Command in Morocco, he was persuaded to accede to Churchill's demand that the Fortresses be given to the British for night bombing. Eaker was furious when told of this decision and threatened to resign his commission so he could take his case to the American people. General Hap Arnold told Eaker that if he felt so strongly about the matter, he himself would arrange a conference between Churchill and Eaker. All America listened in on their radios as Churchill told Parliament, "The British shall bomb at night and the Americans by day, and we shall bomb those devils around the clock."

Ed's father heard the speech while on a Weather Bureau inspection trip and wrote that week, "I am proud of you beyond description not only for what you have done, but for what you are."

Obviously Ed was one of those who took comfort from the decision to concentrate the Fortresses on the purpose for which he had designed them: daylight bombing. In a speech concerning his work on the B-17, Ed recalled the pressures of testing a new design in combat:

> We were building a much larger plane than had been built before in the United States. It was going to have higher performance than any airplane anywhere near that size. The original models had a speed of 240 to 250 miles per hour, which later got up to 275 to 300 miles at altitudes with turbo-superchargers. But a lot of problems had to be solved to make an airplane of that size reliable. There were fuel system problems and control system problems. The fuel system stretched out across an entire wing span. There were changes made in the B-17 constantly during the production runs and these were dictated by whatever experience came back from the combat area. In particular these had to do with armament and placement of guns and types of gun turrets. It led to putting on the chin turret and it also led to the use of armor plating for protection of the crew.
>
> All the systems on the B-17 were originally operated electrically with the exception of the fuel system, which on the experimental Model 299, I used hydraulic drive because of the size of the fuel system, but later models in production used a mechanical fuel pump drive from off the engine. Other than that, the flaps and landing gear and systems of that kind on the airplane were all electrically driven.

Changes and new equipment being demanded by combat experience caused critical problems for Boeing engineers. New equipment required a reassessment of the center of gravity. The aft fuselage had to be rethought, as well as the tail surfaces. The horizontal tail was increased in span by ten feet and the huge dorsal fin was installed. These changes had to be made in midstride, with some- times more than 200 planes a month coming out of the Seattle facto- ry. In his speech, Ed reviewed some of the design problems:

> Early tests indicated that problems could be anticipated if the then avail- able fuel pumps were mounted on the engines as was customary at that time. The length of the fuel lines and the relative location of engines and tanks would restrict the fuel flow unless the pumps could be located near the fuel tank outlets. Thus, a system was developed which included a hy- draulic pump at each tank. An undue number of engineering hours and test hours were expended to make this system work, as the hydraulic motors had an annoying tendency to stall, and, when stopped, failing to become unstuck when pressure was again applied.
>
> The bomb doors were another design problem. Normal operation was by means of electrical actuators, with which we had adequate experience, but there was also a requirement for rapid emergency opening in case of emergency bomb salvo. A number of combinations of gravity, springs and snubbers were tried, but a fully satisfactory solution was not found for the Model 299 which would positively insure emergency opening without the risk of excessive air or inertia loads under some flight condi- tions. The unconventional size and shape of the bomb bay and the doors created this problem, and the unconventional size and shape of the bomb bay was to be the source of another problem later when fuel tanks were required for the bomb bay as an alternate load. In order to fully uti- lize the volume of the bay, the tanks had to be quite deep, with vertical flat sides. A lot of redesign and test hours were expended before a set of tanks could go through the vibration and slosh tests without completely disintegrating. . . .
>
> In 1934, Hamilton Standard offered their new constant speed propeller for the 299. This was a great advance, but we didn't initially understand the problem it posed, particularly when coupled with another new de- vice, the "automatic" mixture control, in the absence of an invention not yet readily available, the torque-meter. . . . In tests of later models with Wright Cyclones and with torque-meters, it was learned that the airplane drag was actually lower than originally estimated, rather than higher as indicated by early tests, but the problem cast a cloud over the airplane for some time. . . . We do learn eventually from experience.
>
> Another problem was that of the tail shimmy. In those days we didn't have as much know-how in hydraulic damping as we have later devel- oped, so initially we used friction damping. I well remember several all- night design and fabrication sessions following the initial taxi tests, try- ing to arrive at a damping arrangement which would stop the shimmy without making the tail wheel completely uncontrollable.
>
> Not only were there some problems to be solved on the initial design, but we also had some classic problems related to design "improve- ments" made on later models.
>
> One of those classic cases was that of the turbo-supercharger installa-

tion, first made on the static test airframe of the Y1B-17A. The original 299 and the basic Y1B-17 had the exhaust outlets on the top of the nacelles, as this was mandatory as a requirement of the current Air Force specification. In making the conversion to turbo-superchargers, this requirement was followed quite literally. But it took only one test flight to show that this was a mistake.

Necessity sometimes is the mother of invention, and in this case a way was soon found to solve a very difficult design problem, getting the turbos and the exhaust outlets off the top of the nacelles, with excellent performance as a result.

Less well known is the classic case of the landing gear. In the original design, it was assumed that the dual-oleo symmetrical design would be superior, particularly for the relatively large wheel, tire and brake to be used. The design was structurally quite satisfactory, but changing the wheels was difficult, since the airplane had to be jacked at a jack point other than the landing gear, with the oleo fully extended, and the axle had to be removed by disconnecting it from the gear at both ends.

Thus, an unsymmetrical stub axle design became a requirement for later models. This was a relatively simple straightforward design, but on one feature we outsmarted ourselves in an attempt to make the structure more determinate. The drag strut was from the front of the nacelle to the lower end of the oleo housing. To prevent the transfer of the loads due to side deflection into the nacelle attachment and into the retracting screw, the shot link was pin-jointed to permit side movement of the oleo relative to the drag strut and the retracting strut. In static tests, however, this neat idea proved to be the undoing of the entire design. Deflecting of the oleo under combined vertical and side loads moved the lower end of the oleo so far to the side and created such an angular deflection in the drag line as to collapse the entire drag structure under an applied end loading. Luckily a quick fix proved to be available, in which a one-piece link replaced the three-piece link and the pin-joint bolts. Sometimes it's better to be simple than too smart.*

By the time the first B-17E was delivered in September 1941, the B-17F, with more than 400 improvements, was already underway. "The B-17F was to become the slickest and highest performance model for the entire B-17 series," wrote Peter Bowers in a manuscript he submitted to Ed Wells. "The G model only added more weight and drag and took performance loss as a result. However, the 'G' gained in combat effectiveness and accounted for more than two-thirds of all B-17's built."

Through all the hundreds of changes, the basic qualities of the original design remained: "We thought it was one of the best ships that ever came across the board," Donald Putt, chief of the Bom-

*Speech before the Seattle chapter of AIAA, October 22, 1974.

A B-17G with war paint (*Boeing 136093B*)

bardment Branch at Wright Field and a survivor of the 299 crash, said in 1943. "It was practically torn apart by the inspection boys, and I don't think there was ever a plane that went through with a better record.

"A good indication of how far ahead of the times it was, is the fact that in nine years it is still basically the same as when it was set down on the drawing board."*

President Franklin Roosevelt had pledged the nation to build 50,000 planes in 1942 and 125,000 in 1943. When the coveted Army and Navy E (for excellence) rating was awarded the company in

*Quoted in *Boeing News*, May 26, 1943.

1942, the *Boeing News* reported that "Boeing has come through with quantity. Since the accelerated procurement, the company has made or exceeded every delivery promise."

When Boeing could not produce Fortresses in the enormous quantity the government demanded, a consortium was set up to turn out the planes as rapidly as possible. It was known as the BVD or "underwear combination," sometimes called the BDV Consortium, because it was made up of Boeing, Vega (Lockheed), and Douglas (both under license from Boeing). Boeing itself turned out 6,981 Fortresses, Lockheed-Vega 2,750, and Douglas 2,995, for a grand total of 12,726 Fortresses during the war. Boeing's assembly was concentrated in Seattle's Plant 2, but over 40 percent of the airframe was subbed out to contractors, including the Boeing plant at Wichita. During the war the Fortress dropped 640,036 tons of bombs on Europe. When the Fortress first took shape on Ed's drawing board in 1934, the company had a payroll of 713. In 1940 this had increased to 8,724, and after the Japanese attacked Pearl Harbor, employment jumped to 28,840, hitting a wartime peak of 44,754 in 1945. Fortresses were being rolled out for delivery from Seattle at the rate of twelve per day, according to Ed, and on a few occasions this number reached sixteen on a single day.

Colonel Frank A. Armstrong, leader of a Flying Fortress bombardment group in Europe, paid a visit to the Boeing plant in Seattle in 1943. He told the Boeing people that "a bomber that is successful in that theater will be successful anywhere. I have seen a big Boeing come home with more than 1,500 holes of small caliber in it, six large 20 millimeter cannon holes and two engines knocked out. My bombardment group made twelve raids before one of the Flying Fortresses was knocked down."

Welcome as was this news, it certainly was not typical in that first year of Fortress raids over Europe.

Colonel Curtis LeMay was insisting that if the factories in Germany could be knocked out, the war could be won without a land invasion. (LeMay had been a lieutenant and navigator on that Fortress "goodwill" mission to Buenos Aires.) At LeMay's urging, two memorable raids were carried out to wipe out the Schweinfurt ball-bearing factory and Regensburg aircraft factory, both deep within Germany. They were executed on August 17, 1943, the anniversary of the first raid with Fortresses on Rouen. LeMay decided to lead the Regensburg effort, which would take his Fortresses across target and over the Alps to his African area of command. The

Schweinfurt raid was described in a 1944 ad for Boeing in these words:

> The bombing mission against Schweinfurt was a battle between large armies, for a crucial objective. The Nazis massed 60 percent of their total fighter strength in a vain effort to prevent the Boeing Flying Fortresses from getting through.
>
> In a period of a few hours the Forts invaded German-held Europe to a depth of 500 miles, sacked and crippled one of her most vital industries. They did it in the daylight and they did it with precision.
>
> They moved in on a city of 50,000 people and destroyed the part of it that contributed to the enemy's ability to wage war. When that part of it was a heap of twisted girders and pulverized machinery, they handed it back, completely useless to the Germans.
>
> This is a task for which the Boeing Flying Fortress was designed: precision destruction by daylight, in areas where the going is toughest. The Fortress is engineered to perform superbly at altitudes of more than 7½ miles; it bristles with effective firepower and it can absorb punishment and still keep fighting. The Germans have even devised special rocket-gun fighters in a vain attempt to drive it from the skies.
>
> Fortresses are lost, of course . . . [a total of 4750 during the entire war].

Despite the damage inflicted on the Germans, the Schweinfurt and Regensburg raids also inflicted Allied losses that could not be sustained. Sixteen percent of the Fortresses sent out on the combined raids were destroyed that day, a casualty rate that if continued would knock out the bomber force in a matter of days.

Jay Spenser, respected aviation historian, has a much different analysis than that of the Boeing publicity department:

> In fact, this mission—the first very deep penetration practiced by the Eighth—was a horrifying failure. It called into question the entire strategic bombardment experiment upon which we had staked all, and which now looked—as the British had confidently predicted—unworkable. The lessons of Schweinfurt were that the Flying Fortress was not a flying fortress; no bomber could survive unescorted in the face of the withering firepower of Hitler's "Festung Europa," which was the hottest theater of World War II. The loss of 60 B-17's (and a number more classed Category E [damaged beyond repair] upon landing) brought about a beneficial reevaluation of how we were waging war, the upshot being the heightening of efforts to develop an escort fighter able to fly all the way to the target and back with bombers.*

*Jay Spenser, letter to the author, February 6, 1989.

These two spectacular raids showed the limits of the B-17s, but they also set a pattern for the war ahead, when bombing would paralyze the German war effort. Germany subsequently dispersed her factories, which increased the need for oil supplies and brought on acute transportation problems. In the end, the Fortresses bombed incessantly. The oil depots, the trains, the trucks were put out of action and Germany was hurting sorely.

Melvin Howard, a reporter and freelance writer, wrote a profile of Ed at the request of *Collier's* magazine in 1943. He sent the manuscript to Ed for corrections and offered his own apology for its flavor, saying the editors were insisting upon "dramatizing you," as this passage of the draft confirms:

> The Axis is bracing for new aerial blows which will spring from the drawing boards of Ed Wells and his fellow engineers at Boeing. . . . It has learned a healthy respect for the "kid engineer." . . . The Reich Marshal Hermann Goering well knows the sting of Edward Curtis Wells' engineering skill and daring. The fierce-eyed, medal-encrusted Goering probably envisages the chief engineer of the Flying Fortress as a ruthless individual who sits up nights thinking up diabolical new bomber turrets for machine-gunning the Luftwaffe pilots in flight.
>
> If Goering were to look up Ed Wells in Seattle tonight, he'd probably find him sitting up, all right, but the chances are that Ed would be discovered perched on a stool in the basement of his home, surrounded by half a dozen squealing youngsters. The kids would be intently watching Engineer Wells punching rows of buttons, putting three electric-powered model trains through a complicated series of maneuvers on 150 feet of criss-cross tracks laid down on a wooden platform which is flanked on one side by a washing machine and on another by several clotheslines.

Perhaps the best description of what Wells was like during the war years comes from his wife, Dorothy, written in response to a request.

> When I told my husband that I had been asked to write an article on being the wife of a famous aviation engineer, his reply was, "Tell them it's terrible. You'd rather not talk about it." I think the best way to tell about being a man's wife is to tell about the man. His work as chief engineer at Boeing Aircraft Company does take a great deal of his time when he is in Seattle, and also requires frequent trips to distant parts. . . .
>
> His administrative duties at the plant take enough of his work so that he works at home on design problems. However, he does all this because he thoroughly enjoys it and is very happy with his work. And hav-

Ed at home with his model railroad (*Boeing H337*)

ing life be a succession of farewells and reunions has its high points as well as low.

And being married to a versatile person with an even disposition, but a tart remark for any occasion, and interesting and thought-provoking views on every subject, certainly has its high points. The best description I know of Ed is in the recent book *Superfortress,* by Tom Collison, wherein Ed is said to be "a quiet genius with a lusty sense of humor."

I feel like bursting with pride when I think he is my husband and see his talents and creative ability reproduced in our children. He is proficient in music, art, contract bridge, tennis, golf, building model railroads and keeping his wife and children in love with him.

In 1943 Ed was promoted to chief engineer, prompting a happy letter from his father.

Mother called me and gave me the good news about the new Chief Engineer. You know, of course, how glad and proud we are, and that our love and good wishes are yours in the new job as they always have been.

I have been thinking of the time, not long after you went to work for the company, when you told me of your ambition to some day be Chief Engineer. Most people would have said such a thing wasn't altogether likely, and I myself didn't know what your chances would be, but I knew you would do your best to merit such an advancement, and that best would be mighty good. Of course, neither of us could know what a very big job this would become.

We do congratulate you, and thank God for the privilege of having such a son.

Will it be o.k. to give an item to the Portland papers about the promotion?

Ed's promotion and increasing fame (in 1942 he received the Lawrence Sperry Award for "outstanding contribution to the art of airplane design") inevitably provoked some hard feelings. After Ed spoke to the Portland Chamber of Commerce about the Flying Fortress in 1944, the father of the late Jack Kylstra approached Ed's father. The elder Kylstra said his son was the real originator of the Flying Fortress and that Ed should not lay claim to it. Wells's father wrote to Ed about the incident, and got a prompt response:

> ...The letter about Mr. Kylstra disturbed me more than just a little. I would like to give you the facts of the matter and perhaps you can relay them to him or I could write him direct if you think I should. Jack did much the same part on the development of the larger XB-15 as I did on the development of the smaller B-17. Although the larger airplane was referred to sometimes as a "Fortress," the name was officially given only to the B-17 series and "Flying Fortress" was made a trademark by The Boeing Company referring to all models of the B-17 series. Jack deserves all the credit anyone can have for his part in the XB-15 development—it just turned out that that development ended with the completion of the first experimental airplane and no further airplanes of this type were built, the interest of the Army having shifted over to the smaller, faster B-17 or "Flying Fortress" series. It is true that Jack was my boss during part of the B-17 development, and I owe a lot to the training that I received from him. However, his primary interest was the XB-15 while mine was the B-17, and it is no wonder that the two are pretty well intermingled in Mr. Kylstra's mind as being "Fortresses." You are certainly right in believing that I have no appetite for publicity. Most of it is sheer mask of words and energy as far as I am concerned, and what little I have put up with has been borne mostly because I felt it was necessary for the best interests of The Boeing Company.

My two sons, both Boeing engineers, also chided me for crediting Ed with the design of the Flying Fortress, saying that a company the size of Boeing just doesn't work that way. But one day my younger son came to me and said, "Mom, I have a big apology to make to you. In the Boeing archives I found the original designs and there's no mistake about it—they were all of them Ed's."

Ed himself, in later life, when I asked how it was possible to design such a plane when he was barely twenty-four, would grin and reply, "Well, there just weren't many people around in those days designing airplanes."

In his speech before the American Institute of Aeronautics and Astronautics, Wells paid tribute to those men who were especially involved in making the Fortress a success. Along with Jack Kylstra, he listed Claire Egtvedt, Fred Laudan, C. N. Monteith, Bob Minshall, Les Tower, Eddie Allen, Wellwood Beall, Maynard Pennell, W. D. Showalter, George Schairer, George Martin, Elliott Merrill, Bill Cook, and "many others."

In 1944, Wells was made "Seattle's Young Man of the Year" by the Junior Chamber of Commerce and the Northwest Commission to Study the Organization of Peace, for "achievement, leadership and service to the community and personal character and ability."

The birthday letter from Ed's father for 1944 focused on the war:

> We continue to read good accounts of the performance of the Fortress. We shall probably need a lot more of them before the war with Japan is over. I can't be as optimistic about the early finish of the war in Europe as some folks are. I hope I am wrong, but I have felt that the Nazis would make a very desperate stand when the war reached Germany, and what is happening on the eastern front seems to bear this out.

But V-E Day did finally arrive. The B-17s had at last convinced Goering and Hitler that it was impossible to go on. Their exhortations would not replace the appalling losses of brave young German pilots shot down by Flying Fortresses and their escorts in thousand-plane sorties.

The next day, Ed's father wrote to congratulate him on his "very important part in hastening" the victory in Europe. Normally as modest as his son, he was bursting with pride and on February 23, 1944, he clipped from *The Oregonian* and sent to Ed the following prediction and words of praise:

> He it is who is credited largely with the design of the Fortress series of American bombers—those giant aircraft that have proved themselves to be so well named. Of the new bomber, the Superfortress, the B-29, which

far succeeds the Flying Fortress in magnitude and range, there is nothing
now to be said. This craft we shall prove on our enemies, as the predecessors have been proved.

No American could possibly have made by his genius a greater contribution to the American cause and victory than has this young
engineer.... When at long last the values are weighed and compared, all
the factors and instruments which gave us the victory, the part played by
the giant bombers of the Boeing Company, whose fighting name ever
shall remain in the American lexicon, doubtless will be seen in all its tremendous significance. We can only guess at it now. Thank you, Mr.
Wells, America thanks you.

In testimony before a congressional committee shortly after the
war ended, Claire Egtvedt explained the critical importance of the
B-17.

The Boeing Flying Fortress occupied a unique and vital role in the war. It
was the only usable land-based airplane available with sufficient range
and in combat condition at the time of the outbreak of the war to aid in
holding back the almost unopposed Japanese naval surge through the
Pacific. The heroic role of these aircraft, few of them as were available,
was highly important in the saving of Australia and sufficient bases from
which to launch a later counterattack.

More important, in the war against Nazi Germany, the Flying Fortress
was the principal key to the breaking up of German industrial might and
Nazi airpower which up to that time had been constantly on the increase.
The solution to this problem lay in the ability to hit the target, deep in
heavily defended Germany. This required daylight operation with the
American precision bombsight—which in turn required an airplane
capable of reaching the target in daylight, through intense opposition,
and getting back again. The Flying Fortress made it possible to begin
this operation in 1942, and, as Germany's own airpower was decreased
thereby, to constantly increase the operation until the time of the German
defeat.

Stacks of magazine articles and newspaper reports and books
have been written concerning the statistics, the glorious triumphs
and miraculous escapes of "The Queen of the Skies," as the Fortress came to be called. There are pictures of their colorful (and
sometimes off-color) names and of the amateurish art with which
some of them were lovingly decorated. There are accounts by the
hundreds of how Fortresses came home full of holes, and on one
sputtering engine as a last hope of power. Some came in with the
tail shot off or a wing hanging on by its skin. There was even a ship
that landed safely in Britain with nobody on board:

There is a documented case of a B-17 landing itself in a field after its crew bailed out. Its wheels and flaps were down to slow it down so there would be minimal dispersion of its crew as they jumped; in this configuration, in a shallow descent, it happened to meet the ground in such a way that it appeared to ground observers to have landed under full control. The incident fueled a rash of eerie tales in the "Flying Dutchman" tradition.*

General Jimmy Doolittle, who later succeeded Ira Eaker as Commander of the Eighth Air Force in England, often related how he owed his life to the fighting power of the Fortress. He and eleven of his staff officers were in flight over Europe when Nazi fighters attacked the plane. When the copilot was wounded, Doolittle helped fly the plane until the Germans were driven off by the American gunners aboard the bomber. "If the Germans had only known who was aboard that plane," the *Boeing News* noted, "they would have been twice as mad at being foiled." Doolittle on a CBS-TV "Air Power" program said, "More than any plane ever built, this plane, the Flying Fortress, had a rendezvous with destiny."

The war with the Nazis was at last over, but the Allies still had to deal with Japan.

*Jay Spenser, personal communication, July 1991.

6

The Superfortress Emerges and Japan Surrenders

America had been caught by surprise by the Japanese attack on Pearl Harbor on December 7, 1941. In Hawaii the military command was asleep at the switch, and in the Philippines—where U.S. forces were also attacked that fateful Sunday morning—MacArthur ordered that the Flying Fortresses at Clark Field, their guns loaded and bomb bays full, could not go into the air to carry out the pre-arranged plan (code name "Rainbow 5") to bomb the Japanese air-bases on Formosa in order to prevent those planes from attacking the Philippines. His reason was that he could not compromise the neutrality of the Philippines or give an order to fire unless fired upon.

Twelve B-17Ds were at Hickam Field in Hawaii on December 7. Fourteen more Fortresses were being flown to Hawaii from the mainland that day. Their bomb bays were carrying extra fuel for the long flight, and in order to lighten the load, all guns and ammunition had been left stateside. These Flying Fortresses arrived defenseless right in the middle of the Japanese attack, their crews believing that the mass of small planes crowding the air space over Honolulu was a welcoming party sent up to greet them.

There were only thirty-five Fortresses in the Philippines that day—nineteen on Clark Field, the rest far to the south on Mindanao. By the end of that day's skirmishing at Clark Field, the B17s had become on-the-ground anti-aircraft stations as airmen turned their Fortress weapons on Japanese Zeros coming in at low altitudes. Finally Bataan, with its "impregnable" Fort Corregidor (which was well supplied with armament but undersupplied with food and medicine), had to give up. MacArthur and his family were flown to Australia in one of the last flyable Flying Fortresses which, had they been spared on December 7, might have saved the Philippines, or at least delayed its surrender.

The few Flying Fortresses that served in the Pacific theater performed gallant service. To quote from Ed Sullivan's syndicated column from the *New York Times* of June 6, 1943:

"The Japs designed the Flying Fortress," Ed Wells will tell you, and the pilots of the Flying Fortress will understand what he means, because the B-17 has been continuously altered as battle conditions demanded changes.

Over Luzon, as history records, the Flying Fortress under Captain Hewitt T. Wheless fought off 18 Jap Zeros while destroying six transports in the harbor. . . . With two engines out of action from cannon hits, a gas tank leaking, all but four control cables shot away, the tail wheel demolished, Wheless got back to base, 400 miles distant. . . . Of his crew one was killed, three badly wounded, all burned by cannon ball fragments. . . . But it got home, Wheless landing on punctured tires. . . . Under Lieutenant General George C. Kenney, the great Fortresses have terrorized the Japs. . . . In the Bismarck Sea battle, the Boeing giants, ignoring a screen of Zeros, handed the Imperial Japanese Navy a flogging from which it never recovered, sinking six transports carrying 15,000 troops and sinking ten protecting Jap warships.

But the range of the B-17 did not allow it to bomb Japan. Racing against time, Boeing was building another bomber to meet that need. During the spring and summer of 1939, Boeing and the Army Air Corps had begun discussions of a "superbomber" with a range of at least 3,000 miles. Meetings at Wright Field involved Ed, Clair Egtvedt, and Wellwood Beall from Boeing, and General Henry "Hap" Arnold, Air Corps Chief, General Frank M. Andrews of GHQ at Langley, Colonel Oliver Echols, in charge of Materiel Command, and Major Donald Putt of Materiel Command's experimental engineering department. Wright Field was urging a plane with a range, if possible, of between 4,000 and 5,000 miles, and Echols said they would accept no sacrifice of speed or armament on this plane.

The Air Corps people were still thinking only in terms of defense of the coastal United States. They wanted to be able to send bombers out to meet an invasion fleet two days' sailing time away from the coasts.

Ed told Echols, "We can put in a lot of armament and cut down on performance, or we can keep performance up and stay out of range of fighter planes. Which do you prefer?"

The colonel's answer, reported by the *Boeing News*, was unyielding: "We've got to have both."

Egtvedt and Ed returned to Seattle deeply worried. High speed and a 5,000-mile range could not be achieved with anything they had so far on the drawing boards. There were severe problems to be solved. Ed and his engineers got busy and turned out a series of paper designs: Model 333-A (January 27, 1939)—range, 3,000 miles, speed, 328 mph at 20,000 feet; Model 333-B (February 21, 1939)— range, 2,500 miles, speed, 364 mph at 20,000 feet; Model 334 (March 4, 1939)—range 4,500 miles, speed 390 mph at 20,000 feet—all models attempting to submerge the engines in the wings in order to cut down on drag.

Then, in July 1939, Ed and his much enlarged staff came up with a design for 334-A, which had an estimated range of 5,333 miles and a possible speed of 390 mph. This would be the design that would evolve into the B-29 Superfortress. The official request from Wright Field to submit proposals on the "superbomber" was still six months away. But Boeing was finally becoming well prepared to submit its bid with Model 341, designed between August 1939 and March 1940, with a range of 5,333 miles at design gross weight and 7,000 miles at maximum alternate gross weight, and a speed of 405 mph at 25,000 feet. All of Boeing's accumulation of experience went into this design, to make it, as the engineers were saying, "aerodynamically cleaner than has ever been built before."

Boeing was committed to the design and began a full-scale wooden model of the plane at company expense. But Model 341 was getting precariously heavy, and its plan of armament was questionable since it consisted of four remote-controlled retractable turrets with guns sighted through periscopes, which now had to be abandoned if the plane was to have both speed and range. There could not even be a rivet that was not flush with the surface, and retractable turrets posed a huge aerodynamic problem.

In January 1940, President Roosevelt asked Congress for an appropriation of $300 million for plane purchase. Boeing came up with a design for an even larger bombing plane, naming it Model 345. Some said the difference between it and the 341 was the intensity with which the war was being fought in Europe, and the discouraging losses inflicted by the Nazis. On January 29, 1940, a letter marked "R-40-B" was dispatched from the office of Colonel Putt to aircraft companies, asking for the submission of proposals on the "superbomber." Ironically, bad flying weather delayed delivery of Boeing's copy until the first week in February.

The Army Air Forces' performance specifications called for a range of 5,333 miles (the exact range of Boeing's Model 334-A). All designs would have to be submitted and received by Materiel Command within thirty days, and the airplane must be completed and delivered by August 3, 1942. "This airplane was to be the big jump," wrote Tom Collison in *The Superfortress*, "indeed a range, speed and bomb load jump that normally would have taken five years. These men were short of everything but personal skill, experience and courage; short of facilities, skilled personnel in numbers, short of time."

Sometime in March 1940 a supplementary specification was sent to Boeing asking for additions to the design: leakproof fuel tanks and additional armament. The deadline for submission of designs was extended. On May 11, 1940, Boeing submitted its Model 345 drawings to Wright Field. To Model 341, they had added seventeen more feet in wing span and eight feet in length. It had an estimated speed of 382 mph, but still with retractable gun turrets (required by Wright Field) with eight .50 caliber machine guns, one 20mm cannon and two .50 caliber machine guns in the tail. It required 1,270 more gallons of fuel than Model 341.

In January 1940, President Roosevelt asked Congress for an appropriation of $1 billion: $100 million additional for national defense. And General Arnold called for all aircraft leaders to meet with him on May 20 to discuss defense plans and how to get organized. Wells was at that meeting.

Early in June 1940 the War Department authorized the expenditure of $85,652 to be given to Boeing to provide more design data and for the construction of wind tunnel models. On June 27 came the official contract and more money for the building of a full-scale wooden mock-up of Model 345, which was now given the official Air Force designation of XB-29.

The B-29 would have a pressurized cabin; a tricycle landing gear with a double-wheel arrangement; larger wing flaps than ever had been tried before (constituting one-fifth of the wing area); two turbo-superchargers on each of its four engines; far greater range, speed, and bomb capacity than any plane built thus far; and greater flexibility between carrying bombs and fuel load. It would have to be able to fly to Japan, lay down its bombs and return. Fly from China? From the Marianas, if they could be captured? That would remain to be seen.

The B-29 represented the most extensive engineering progress in aerodynamic research and flight analysis ever achieved. And as an

The secret XB-29 high altitude bomber of 1942 (*Boeing X-6*)

editorial in the August 17, 1964, *Wichita Eagle* acknowledged: "When things go wrong and development falters, the team is not castigated. It is the engineering leader who has his valves ground." Ed was only twenty-eight when he began to assume responsibility for the B-29. However, he had the assistance of the best specialists in aerodynamics and testing in the persons of George Schairer and Eddie Allen, and the technical and financial development of the company between 1936 and 1940 laid the groundwork for this ambitious job.

The Air Force examined the results of wind tunnel testing, and on August 24, 1940, they signed a contract of two XB-29s for $3,615,095. In November two more were ordered, one of them for test-to-destruction use.

The most critical design problem remaining involved the retractable turrets required by Wright Field. Jake Harman and Roger Williams, who was in charge of the armament section at Wright Field, came to Seattle in December 1941 to demand, under orders from General Kenneth B. Wolfe, that Boeing use locally controlled, retractable turrets on the B-29. Ed and his men explained how this would spoil the aerodynamics of the plane, affecting range, speed, and other factors. Retractable turrets also would make it impossible

Mockup of the XB-29 used to test design configuration (*Boeing 15781B*)

to pressurize the cabin, forcing the crews to use oxygen throughout the long flights.

Nevertheless, Wolfe threatened to break both men to worse than second lieutenants if they didn't come back with an agreement from Boeing to install the turrets. Then Williams suggested a way out of the impasse. General Electric had developed a system of electronic remote control firing. Rather than submitting to the narrow visual field of a periscope, gunners could scan the skies and aim their sights, and electronic tubes would reproduce the movements in the guns. This system was perfected in a joint effort of Air Technical Service Command, General Electric, and Boeing, and the aerodynamic streamlining of the B-29 was saved.

Although guns could be fired by remote control, there was no way to launch bombs without opening bomb bays. The problem of maintaining pressurization in the crew cabin was solved by pressurizing only the front and rear crew compartments plus a narrow tunnel over the bomb bays that connected the two. After Japan entered the war, kapok was no longer available for insulation, and hair and cotton were too heavy. Fiberglass was found to be an excellent substitute. The turbo-superchargers were adapted to provide air-conditioning and pressurization.

Wichita was chosen as the main focus of assembly for B-29s, but the floor space in all Boeing facilities would have to expand enormously to build Fortresses and Superfortresses simultaneously. Boeing Plant 2 at Seattle grew to 1,778,000 square feet; Plant 1 to 319,000 square feet; Plant 3 to 182,500 square feet; Wichita Plant 1 to 300,000 square feet; Wichita Plant 2 to 440,000 square feet; and Boeing of Canada, in Vancouver, to 326,000 square feet. By 1940 there were 3,509,500 square feet in the Boeing facilities, five times the area Boeing owned when the war started. The new facilities at Wichita would cost $3.5 million.

The first B-29 Superfortress was rolled out for ground tests of all systems in September 1942, missing its original delivery deadline by only a few weeks. On May 17 of that year, Colonel William F. Volandt, contract officer for the Air Force, had forwarded this letter to Phil Johnson at Boeing:

> The War Department anticipates placing an order with you for approximately the following airplanes, funds for which, in the amount of ten million dollars, are available at this time.
>
> 250 B-29 airplanes
> 335 additional B-17 type airplanes
>
> Procurement is conditioned upon expansion of facilities at Boeing-Wichita to permit monthly production capacity of sixty-five B-17 and twenty-five B-29 airplanes by July 1, 1942, and February 1, 1943, respectively.
>
> The Secretary of War advises that in the interest of national defense it is necessary that production be not delayed, awaiting the placing of the aforesaid order or orders. You will hereby be authorized to purchase such jigs, dies and fixtures (except machine tools and production machines) and such critical material and equipment as are necessary to the production of such aircraft and spare parts in anticipation of the placing of such order or orders.

Now was the time for flight-testing. Eddie Allen had told the Air Force that it would take 200 hours of flight-testing over four or five months before the plane could be delivered. The first test flight was successful. Eddie Allen's evaluation was succinct: "She flies." Then there began to be problems—serious ones—with the Wright engines and other equipment. Boeing was not responsible for the engine functioning during the tests, but it was fatally bound by any malfunction. On December 30, during a test of B-29 number 2, there was a fire in an engine. Smoke filled the cockpit when the fire

The B-29 (*Boeing BW34367*)

could not be put out. With consummate skill and a lot of luck Eddie Allen brought the plane in, and the men jumped to safety.

On February 4, 1943, Phil Johnson was presiding over a staff meeting. The B-29 was aloft in another test flight. The telephone rang in the outer office. Ed excused himself to answer it. It was the control tower. He came back with the color drained from his face, saying that Eddie was coming in with a wing on fire. They never made it. An engine had caught fire. They had been able to put out that fire, but as they were coming in low over downtown Seattle, another engine started to burn. Pieces of burning magnesium burned holes in the wing and the fuel tanks ignited. The plane hit the Frye meat packing plant, killing all twelve on board, plus nineteen employees of the packing plant.

As a memorial to Eddie Allen, Boeing named the Edmund T. Allen Wind Tunnel and Aeronautical Research Laboratories just south of Plant 2. Ed grieved sorely. He had treasured the man.

The bomber was too important to the nation and its survival for anything more to happen to the program at this point. Jake Harman went to General Wolfe and proposed that a special department be set up to push through flight-testing and production. The two men thought that General Arnold himself should head up a special B-29 program, as an independent force that could operate from advance bases against the Japanese. Arnold's final response was, "Approved. Plan it for you-know-where." "Where" was going to be India, on to bases set up in unoccupied China, and "bombs away" over Tokyo.

But first the planes had to be built, with parts subcontracted out all over the United States and the whole coordinated into what was to be known as "The Battle of Kansas."

The miracle was achieved. Untrained people were brought to Wichita and Seattle from all over the United States to put the B-29 together with parts manufactured from all over the United States. They succeeded in sorting out the parts, learning the skills, and braving the weather, hot or cold. Somehow they got the planes turned out for the thousands of pilot trainees who, too, were brought to Kansas air bases from all over the United States to go through one of the most rigorous training programs ever conceived.

On the other side of the world, in India and in Chengtu, China (territory the Japanese had not yet appropriated), bases were built to receive the B-29s. A crew of almost half a million Chinese workers was recruited to build the airstrips at Chengtu. No cement or tar was available—just hand-hewn rock, cut and carried and fitted, piece by piece, until the long runways were smooth and solid and ready to receive the giant planes.

The first B-29 was sent as a decoy to Europe over the North Atlantic route, while Jake Harman led the first real delivery across to North Africa and on to the new base in India. The flight was supposed to be classified, but the Japanese learned of it and Tokyo Rose announced it to the world. The planes landed in India on April 7, 1944. When they had ferried enough bombs and fuel to India and China, they could attempt that first raid on Japan: from India about 1,200 miles over the Himalayas to China, a refueling and sleep, then take off for Japan. This would be a flight of 5,600 miles round trip, with luck and weather permitting.

What little time Ed had for himself during this period was still spent with the children and his model trains. The first house on Cascadia Avenue was now bulging at the seams, and the family bought another one just down the street. It was a large Colonial-style brick house with a larger basement.

Ed now had both "O" gauge trains and "HO" models. Soon he would buy a tiny "TT" train to run in a circle track around a small table-top Christmas tree, surrounded by a Norwegian village with evergreen trees fashioned from curled wood shavings.

Since vacations away from Seattle were not possible because of the demands on Ed's time, the Wellses rented a small summer cottage on Lake Meridian south of Seattle. Here Ed could come home from work every day, spend time with the children, and teach them to swim. During all this time, Ed was having to fly often to Washington, D.C., and Wichita for consultation and supervision. Dorothy's "farewells and reunions" were getting to be a regular part of the household schedule.

In February 1945, Ed flew to Philadelphia to receive the Fawcett Aviation Award for 1944, given "to the person making the greatest single contribution during the year to the scientific advancement of aviation as a public service." The award was sponsored by Fawcett Publications, which had profiled Ed in the April 1944 issue of one of its magazines, *Mechanix Illustrated*. The article itself had been somewhat inept, beginning with the misjudgment that "he's so shy and retiring that hardly anyone will realize he's at the party till it's breaking up," and then offering the consolation that "if he is colorless and unimpressive in appearance and deportment, Ed Wells is a sparkling demon over the drawing board." The award would be presented during a national radio program and "would be good publicity for Boeing." Travel was an unwelcome complication in an already overcrowded schedule, but it did provide one unexpected pleasure, reported in the June 1945 edition of the *Boeing News:*

> On a Philadelphia corner, one evening, Wells was waiting for a taxi to take him to the broadcast of "We, The People." There, on a Columbia Broadcasting national hookup, he was to receive the 1944 Fawcett Aviation Award.

After a long time a taxi appeared, but a woman hopped into it before Wells could. He opened the door, explained his problem and asked for a lift.

"Rawther!" said the woman, and that is how Ed Wells rode to the broadcast with the famous Beatrice Lillie. Miss Lillie, it turned out, was on the same program. And while Wells is convinced that the surest way to get somewhere quickly is on a C-97, you can't always meet Beatrice Lillie that way.

In China, preparations were being intensified for the first long-range bombing of mainland Japan. On April 18, 1942, Lieutenant Colonel Jimmy Doolittle had led a daring raid from an aircraft carrier upon Japan itself to let them know we *would* do it. (Soon B-29s would prove we *could* do it.) Jay Spenser describes Doolittle's raid as "perhaps the single most dramatic mission flown by the U.S. Army Air Forces during WW II. Coming less than four months after Pearl Harbor, during the darkest days of the war when it seemed there was nothing to stop the Japanese from reaching American shores, it was a tremendous morale booster. The tiny bit of damage done to specific military targets in Tokyo, Nagoya and Kobe pales into insignificance beside all that unbelievably daring and imaginative raid did to hearten America."[*]

Now that the B-29s were ready for combat, a preliminary strike to test their strength was made on the shipping facilities in the harbor at Bangkok. Next it would be war in earnest over mainland Japan. The target would be the vast steel mills at Yawata on June 14, 1944.

General Wolfe had hoped to lead this raid on Japan because he was now in command in China. He was bitterly disappointed when he received orders that those in command were forbidden to take part in a raid. Jake Harman was to lead it, but his plane malfunctioned when it was airborne and, brokenhearted, he had to return to base. The raid itself was a success—involving more than sixty planes—with few losses incurred: two planes crashed on takeoff; another probably was lost over Yawata with crew and a *Newsweek* correspondent on board; and another had to "ditch" over occupied China with a *Time* correspondent aboard. The *Time* reporter and crew were able to find their way back to base after a few days.

Elated by this success, General Arnold announced from Wash-

[*]Jay Spenser, letter to the author.

ington that "this employment of the B-29 makes possible the softening-up attack on Japan very much earlier than would be possible with aircraft hitherto known to combat. This mighty weapon advances the bomber line a long way.... They can strike from many and remote bases at a single objective."

The raids on Japan continued, with hits at Sasebo Naval Base, Anshan, and Nagasaki. Then Saipan, Tinian, and Guam were at last captured by the United States forces. These forward bases would make it possible to bomb Japan almost at will. In August Major General LeMay took command in the Marianas. Ed was summoned to go to the Marianas for consultation on the B-29s stationed there, with a view of improving their performance for more raids on Japan. He was given the rank of colonel, to be rescinded at the completion of the trip.

The trip was necessary because the B-29s were not performing up to expectations. "The flight crews were not satisfied with the available operating charts and the accuracy thereof," Ed noted in his diary of the trip. "It was felt that the bomb load might be increased by operational refinements."

Ed summed up the goal of his visit succinctly: "Object: to increase the ratio of bombs to gasoline carried for missions over Japan." Ed was part of a team of engineers—Elliott Merrill and J. D. Alexander of Boeing, and M. R. Hall of Wright Field—who made the trip to the Marianas. They began their evaluations en route by making the flight in a fully instrumented B-29. Wells kept a meticulous record of the trip. The group left Mather Field in California on March 7, 1945, landing in Honolulu ten hours, thirteen minutes later. The next leg of the journey was from Honolulu to Kwajalein, Marshall Islands, and then on to Guam.

"The first several days on Guam were spent talking with the 21st Bomber Command personnel and trying to set up a test program," Ed wrote. "While holding these discussions the airplane underwent a 50-hour inspection. The turbine wheel had radial cracks, extending into the bucket blades themselves." The project gave Ed a welcome opportunity to discuss the planes with the people who flew and cared for them. "Wells disappeared repeatedly," an *Aero Digest* reporter wrote in February 1951, "to be found hours later hashing over maintenance problems with a line chief or ground crew."

Wells considered the six-week trip a success. His report concluded:

The B-29 is now starting to give the results that have been hoped for during the last few years. The bomb load is approaching the maximum and the destruction wrought on the Japanese homeland is tremendous. This change has been due to the gradual improvement of the airplane and power plant, not only along service lines but also operational procedures. By the adoption of the operational procedures recommended herein, the fuel consumption can be reduced as much as 7.5 percent at cruising power and the flight engineer can estimate his fuel consumption to as close as 2 percent. This figure was obtained from a check on six combat airplanes flying to Tokyo and return.

The process of learning in action shows up in Ed's summary of the B-29 missions over Japan. Phase one missions, which continued until January 1945, involved bombing from around 30,000 feet. The bombing accuracy was "very poor," due to the altitude and the unexpected winds at that altitude.

Phase two missions reduced the weight of the B-29s by removing the armor plating and other extras, and reduced the altitude to 25,000 feet. Greater accuracy and a heavier bomb load resulted, but fighter opposition was reported as "very heavy."

Phase three brought the formations into wings. "The 313 Wing started into combat at this time from Tinian. One group of the 313th Wing suffered terrific losses on its first raid. One plane was lost on takeoff, two collided near the target, one was lost due to enemy action and four planes were ditched. Eight airplanes were lost out of a group of sixteen."

Phase four was a response to changing weather conditions. In order to avoid flying in formation through a cloud bank, the bombers flew single-ship until they reached bombing altitude, then made a group formation.

Phase five started in early March, with night bombing from about 7,000 feet. "This type of raid has been very satisfactory and resulted in heavy destruction of the Japanese homeland. Opposition from night fighters and flak was not severe. However, the airplanes at this low altitude do get into the thermals caused by fires below. The unstable air is very severe and the B-29s are bounced around considerably. Some reported doing spins, rolls and even Immelmanns. . . . This type of mission can be expected to continue until the Japanese can prepare adequate defense."

The lower altitude made it possible to more than double the bomb load, to about 15,000 pounds.

Phase six began with the capture of Iwo Jima. Daylight missions from the Marianas picked up fighter escort from Iwo Jima, and bombed from 15,000 feet. "At this altitude the accuracy appears to be very good."

Reducing the bombing altitude meant considerable fuel savings. The "absorption rate" (airplanes returning before reaching target) decreased by almost half, and the time between engine overhauls increased about 40 percent.

Wells also made a quick flight from Guam to Iwo Jima, which after its capture was used as an emergency field for B-29s as well as a launching area for fighter escort.

> Some B-29's land there that really have no apparent reason for doing so, aside from not knowing their actual fuel reserve. The advent of the new fuel flow charts and future installation of flowmeters will eliminate a great many B-29 stops at Iwo Jima. Many others land there out of necessity. One particular B-29 was observed on Iwo Jima that had been shot up over Tokyo. It had been rammed by an enemy fighter. The fighter had gone through the number 3 propeller and bent it back over the nacelle, and had continued on, shearing off about half of the vertical stabilizer. This B-29 came into Iwo Jima with wheels down and it will be repaired to fly again another day. The crews are amazed how the B-29 can take such tremendous punishment and yet fly home or at least to Iwo.

Ed also noted some personal reactions concerning Iwo Jima: "What a place! Dirt, dust, cinders, smells, death and destruction. The earth steams. . . . Ate K-rations for lunch. On our own for a couple of hours. Wandered around picking up souvenirs." On their return to Seattle the Boeing men summed up Iwo Jima as "a good place not to be."

The work party returned to the States on April 22, six weeks and 35,000 miles later. They were welcomed as heroes back in Seattle, and, of course, Dorothy was immensely relieved.

"Boeing B-29s will be in demand all the way to the finish in the war against Japan and with each shortening of the road to Tokyo will pack a mightier punch," reported the June 1945 *Boeing News.*

"Those pilots over there have been asked to do a big job and they're pitching in and doing it," Ed said. "It's a long ride those crews are going on, sometimes up to 22 hours in the air."

During Ed's tour, General LeMay had, against all advice to the contrary, decided to use incendiary bombs to destroy Tokyo and all of its widespread small war-manufacturing facilities. The B-29s were stripped of their armor and all armament was left behind. The planes went in individually at low altitudes to set fire to the great city. It was costly, but it worked, and the pilots returned with praise for the B-29. "Part of the force of over 300 Superfortresses which attacked the Japanese capital in the dark hours before dawn, the crews of four B-29's were jubilant not only at the success of their first combat mission, but because their planes functioned perfectly," wrote St. Clair McKelway. One of the pilots said, "I've flown a lot of Boeing Flying Fortresses, and always thought they were fine planes, but the B-29 beats 'em all."*

Then on August 6, a B-29 called *Enola Gay* (after the pilot's mother) put on board that enormous lethal egg called "the atomic bomb" and took off from Tinian and dropped the egg on Hiroshima. Another B-29 dropped another of these mystery bombs over Nagasaki three days later to end the war.

The *Portland Journal* wrote in an editorial:

> If that boy of yours insists on drawing models of airplanes, boats or motors on the walls of home, sweet home, don't revive the modern version of the old-fashioned razor strop and the woodshed. Encourage him. Give him a drawing board. He may be getting ready to help win the war with weapons more powerful than guns. Namely, ideas. He may be another Edward C. Wells.

---

*St. Clair McKelway, "A Reporter with the B-29s," *New Yorker*, June 9, 16, 23, and 30, 1945.

7

Into the Future with Jet Planes

In *Flying Fortress*, Thomas Collison has written, "The aeronautical engineer is a hero who has scaled the heights; the person who gives us the machines that enrich our lives in peacetime; the man who gives us highly destructive and complex instruments to protect us from our enemies in time of war."

During the war, an article in *Mechanix Illustrated* (April 1944) said, "Ed Wells, as an aeronautical engineer, has affected the destiny of nations," but after Hiroshima some labeled him "the creator of the deadliest weapon of World War II." Of course the atom bomb was the deadly weapon, but it was Ed's bomber that dropped the bombs. And during the Pacific phase of the war, Boeing's Superfortresses (B-29s) had dropped another 171,000 tons of conventional bombs on Japanese targets, and by August 1945, the United States government had accepted from Boeing and others of the consortium 3,960 B-29s to deliver those bombs.

But Ed Wells was a gentle man, fiercely committed to peace. He followed faithfully the tradition of his paternal grandfather and of his father, who refused to have a gun in house or in hand. Each had said, "A gun in the house may kill someone." Just as a skilled surgeon who uses a knife to excise a cancerous growth is hardly a butcher, so Ed saw the weapons of war in the air as a means of excising the cancerous Axis threat to the freedoms in the world. And he grieved over the waste of lives and materials in such an excision. He looked forward eagerly to the day when his engineers and all of Boeing could devote their hours and their talents to designing and building commercial transports which might bring the world together in closer understanding.

"We welcome this opportunity to turn towards peacetime accomplishments," he said in a speech after the war. "Although a contribution to national defense is important and necessary, it will always be, in a sense, a negative accomplishment. The commercial jet age offers us almost unlimited opportunity for a constructive contribution to the national and regional welfare. It is also a tremendous competitive challenge which we accept with enthusiasm."*

In 1945 Boeing was in another period of crisis. Phil Johnson had died of a stroke on September 14, 1944, while visiting the Boeing plant in Wichita. Claire Egtvedt took over temporarily while a search was made for a new president. Then the war ended and the American military had less need for the rush of B-29s coming out of the factories. On September 5, 1945, the government canceled a contract for 5,000 B-29s. Boeing's payroll was $500,000 per day, and there were no orders for commercial planes in sight. Employment dropped from 35,000 to 6,000 in Seattle and from 16,000 to 1,500 in Wichita.

William Allen, longtime legal counsel for Boeing, was approached about taking the presidency. He said he felt unqualified for the job. Mary Ellen Agen, a neighbor who later became his wife, is reported to have told him that if the company had decided they thought him qualified, who was he to say otherwise? Finally, Allen reluctantly took over, on the same day the B-29 contract was canceled.

Allen called Ed in and quizzed him about the possibility of getting more orders for the new B-50 bombers. Ed said that although the B-50s were much lighter and stronger than the B-29s from which they had evolved, the two planes still looked too similar, and the Air Corps was already overloaded with B-29s. Then Wells said he had an idea for a new approach. Allen's response to Ed's request for a hearing on a jet plane was abrupt: "We need something we can build and sell right now."

In fact Boeing's situation did look grim. In a speech made in 1974 to the Wings Club in New York, Wells recalled an exchange between Allen and one of his managers during contract negotiations after the postwar crisis had passed. The manager said, "Look, Mr. Allen, it's hard for you to understand this because you started out at the top—not the bottom."

Allen reared back and thundered, "Top! Top! I'll have you know that when I started out it was all bottom!"

*"The Jet Age," speech to the Men's Club, University Temple, September 1956.

Senior project engineer A. I. Ostlund and Ed with a model of the B-50, 1946 (*Boeing P6352*)

In 1945, Allen could not afford to finance development of a jet, or to wait for it to be ready. He decided to push for construction of the Model 377 Stratocruiser, a commercial version of the C-97 Stratofreighter military transport plane. Ed described it as a plane weighing seventy tons, "double-decked, a 300 to 340 mile-per-hour luxury transport, completely air conditioned, cruising at altitudes of 15,000 to 25,000 feet with a maximum range of 4,000 miles, normally carrying 75 passengers, and including a lower deck lounge." The Stratocruiser was expensive. Boeing would have to sell at least fifty to begin to make a profit, and Allen announced that "the job

The 377 Stratocruiser, commercial version of the C-97. (*Boeing P8186*)

for everybody here is to get out and sell them!" His high hopes were realized. The airlines contracted for forty-two and promised to buy more.

Boeing was not the only part of the aircraft industry in crisis just after the war. Congress was holding inquiries and the Defense Department was getting ready to establish the Air Force as a separate entity.

At the heart of the issue was the government's role in peacetime. Egtvedt had already in 1945 testified before the Mead Committee of Congress, whose mandate was to determine what level of aircraft development and production was needed to retain the skills and facilities developed during the war. Egtvedt urged that what was learned during the war should be encouraged and retained. He also told Congress that military development in peacetime could save money in the long run:

> Notice from the following figures how much more engineering is called for after an airplane gets into large scale military operations than in the original design:

YB-17 (13 airplanes)	121,000 engineering manhours
B-17B (39 airplanes)	281,000 engineering manhours
B-17C&D (80 airplanes)	263,000 engineering manhours
B-17E (500 airplanes)	557,000 engineering manhours
B-17F&G (several thousand)	3,756,000 engineering manhours
XB-29 (experimental model)	1,432,000 engineering manhours
B-29 (production model)	6,133,000 engineering manhours

(For rough conversion, 1,000,000 manhours equals about 500 years with a 40-hour week)

Egtvedt ends his plea with this paragraph:

An investment in "insurance" through development and procurement of the most advanced equipment in peacetime years may prove the lowest cost to the nation in the long run. The cost to the United States of engaging in World War II has been stated as $287,181,000,000. If a heavier peacetime expenditure could have provided sufficient defensive power to dissuade the aggressors from embarking upon war, how tremendous would have been the saving in dollars and lives.

John D. Vandercook, a popular news commentator, broadcast the same message on August 29, 1947. In his remarks about President Truman's Air Policy Commission, he used the career of Ed Wells as his example:

Since 1933, Eddie Wells has had a hand in the creation and design of every plane built by Boeing, from the first two-engine transport to the newest Stratocruiser now being tested for scheduled airline service. Mr. Wells is part of a tightly organized team of engineers, designers and production men who conceive a new airplane and eventually make it a reality by almost a magical series of operations. . . . Since the war, Eddie Wells had seen his staff, his team, dwindle from 5,000 to 2,000 men. And with the departure of each man for other employment, goes knowledge and experience and ability which may be lost to aviation forever. That human side of airplane making is something the President's air policy seekers might well look into, for the condition is not peculiar to any one company. The accumulated know-how these youthful designers and engineers carry in their heads is just as important to the future of our aircraft program as is the question of who is going to pay for the development of new transport and military planes. You just don't buy that kind of brains at the corner store. But back to Eddie Wells . . . he weighs his words carefully, a trait that comes from doing a job where a poor guess could cost millions. But I believe Mr. Wells could tell the air policy board makers a thing or two. He could tell them of the great necessity for keeping the design and engineering staffs of our aircraft industry intact when we are

seeking the answer to what we will need today and tomorrow to safe-
guard our place in the skies.

Ed testified on national air policy before the Mitchell Committee
on June 3, 1946. He urged a continuation of the cooperation between the three elements of "Air Power": the air force or government, air commerce, and the aircraft industry:

> Faced by the emergency of World War II, the three elements of Air Power
> embarked upon a cooperative effort which was... eminently suc-
> cessful... and each progressed technologically to a new threshold of
> achievement.
>
> Arrival at that threshold came concurrently with the end of hostilities.
> New military tactics and equipment were almost, but not quite ready for
> experimentation—new fields of research and development were almost,
> but not quite ready for exploration—new applications of craft and safety
> equipment were almost, but not quite ready for use—and new design
> and manufacturing techniques were almost, but not quite ready for uni-
> versal application.
>
> With V-J Day, the impetus provided by the war emergency was re-
> moved, and with it went the compelling urge for the utmost in coordi-
> nation and teamwork.... We need an effective means of planning and
> coordinating our activities which will take the place of the instinct for
> cooperative self-preservation which exists only during a national emer-
> gency....
>
> It seems obvious that we will not be able to continue spending our re-
> sources at a wartime rate. It, therefore, also seems obvious that the ex-
> penditures we do make should be so planned as to give the maximum of
> return.
>
> Let us take the example in the field of engineering development and
> research. We are on the threshold of significant discoveries relating to
> transonic and supersonic flight. Wartime developments brought us to
> that point, but at the same time these developments have also brought us
> face to face with the realization of the magnitude of the problems which
> are as yet unsolved. Neither government alone, nor industry alone can
> provide the high degree of technical skill nor the tremendous facilities
> which will be required to carry us very far beyond our present state of
> knowledge. Each of the agencies concerned has made proposals concern-
> ing facilities required for supersonic development and research. There is
> no one agency at present qualified to pass upon the suitability of such
> proposals on long range terms. Nor has sufficient thought been given to
> the fact that facilities without proper direction and without trained and
> skilled operating personnel will not produce results commensurate with
> the cost.
>
> As it is in the field of supersonic development and research so it is in
> other related fields, such as materials, structures, power plants, equip-
> ment, aids to safety, communication and navigation facilities. In each we

have uncovered new possibilities and new and greater unsolved problems. . . .

Much has been said of the Morrow Board, and I think that you will all agree that we are thankful to the gentlemen of that board for the effective manner in which they accomplished their task in 1925. I am sure that you will also agree that conditions have changed in the ensuing 21 years, requiring a new statement of this country's Air Policy. I know that it is the sincere belief of most engineers that changes in the next 21 years, or even the next 5 years may well outstrip the changes that have taken place in the last 21 years.

These technological advancements will be given impetus by the establishment of a fair, but positive Air Policy for the United States. This policy, and the means of providing effective coordination of activities in support of such a policy, can best be established and maintained by an impartial, qualified, National Air Policy Board.

Above all, our Air Policy, when established, should recognize that we are on the threshold of significant engineering and scientific advancements, and should therefore be adapted to change as required, for the full exploitation in the national interest, of all such advancements.

Following the hearings, President Truman appointed Thomas Finletter as chairman of the Air Policy Commission.

The development of jet airplanes provided ample documentation of the need for postwar cooperation in air power. Ed's own interest went back to the time when the B-29 was first going into production. One day there came "a cryptic phone call asking me to report without delay to Edwards Air Force Base, 'no questions asked.' There, I was to see the first Bell experimental jet fighter demonstrated in flight, a most impressive sight, to be sure. Thanks to Sir Frank Whittle (its inventor), we were now to have a jet engine on which we could base a whole new generation of airplanes.*

After the war ended, Ed and George Schairer went to work on the jet idea, hoping they could get a design on the drawing board, a design that neither Wright Field nor William Allen could refuse. Finally Allen, still somewhat reluctant, gave Ed the go-ahead, saying, "If that's what you really want, let's go for it."

Wells put together a project group, naming his old friend George Martin in charge. Martin and Schairer had been sent to Germany on two separate commissions of investigation of aviation matters just after the surrender of the Axis powers. There they picked up some ideas for swept-wing configuration and jet power. The ideas had

---

*Speech accepting the Tony Jannus Award, March 1985.

been around for some time, mentioned in scientific meetings, but had not been taken too seriously.

On September 13, 1945, Martin sent Wright Field a formal proposal which called for a swept-wing bomber with four jet engines in the wings and two in the tail. Swept wings could attain higher speeds, as sweep delays the onset of compressibility. Firewalls were added to address the Air Corps's objection to engines in the body of the plane. (Fuselage and tail engines would later give way to wing-mounted engines.)

Back at Wright Field, Boeing found only one friend for their proposal—Colonel "Pete" Warden, the bombardment project officer. The firewalls were not enough to reassure the other men. Wright's armament laboratory had test-fired .50-caliber bullets into the burner section of a jet engine, and the resulting firestorm had made an impression on the staff. Ed and Bob Jewett, who had come to Dayton to receive the verdict, were discouraged as they went back to the Van Cleve Hotel, the "home away from home" for Boeing engineers on trips to Wright Field. They began to ask themselves very critical questions. Suddenly Ed thought, "I've never been happy with the engines in the body. Why not place them out away from the wing?"

He remembered some wind tunnel reports Schairer had brought back from Germany, and he started to draw out a new configuration for his jet plane. They hurried back to Seattle where Schairer could wind-tunnel their ideas.

Just as George Schairer had made those successful wind tunnel tests on many wing configurations until he came upon the correct thin swept-back configuration used for the B-47, he began now, at Ed's request, to make wind tunnel tests to find where to place jet engines outside the wings. Boeing called these the "broomstick tests," since dummy engines were mounted on the ends of sticks of various lengths and placed in front of, above, and below the wing. According to the wind tunnel, below and in front of the wing proved to be the optimum position. At this point the drag was no greater than having the engines in the body. Four engines in twin pods would be slung under and in front of the wings and two engines would be placed out near the tips of the wings. Besides improving safety, this configuration increased the plane's range by reducing its weight.

With the new design, the plane could be expected to make more than 600 mph. Wright-Patterson became enthusiastic, but not for long. In April 1946, this jet bomber, called by Boeing "the Stratojet," was a full-scale wooden mockup and the Air Corps was invited to come to look at it. They said if this was the best Boeing could do, they might have to reconsider the whole project. Ed, Martin, and Schairer began hurriedly "to fix what was wrong." They substituted a bicycle landing gear with wheels in tandem, and added small outrigger wheels to keep the wing tips off the ground. These changes took off another 3,000 pounds, and range consequently increased. Then, at the insistence of the Air Corps, the wing-tip engines were also placed on pods, which necessitated increasing the wing span by sixteen feet. Ed and Martin knew that the Stratojet was "right," and soon Wright-Patterson approved a contract for the production of two experimental models to be known as the XB-47.

Just at the time that Boeing was hurrying to meet delivery on these two aircraft, the company got word from Wright-Patterson that they had won the competition for the design study on a long-range bomber in the "heavy" class, a giant plane powered by turboprop engines, a plane which would weigh at least twice as much as the Stratojet.

Boeing's design called for a 360,000-pound plane with a 3,110-mile range at 450 mph. The plane was heavier and the range less than the Air Force specifications, but it came nearest. According to Lieutenant Colonel Richard L. Geer, Boeing won the design competition against Martin and Consolidated Vultee "on the basis of best performance per dollar cost and the company's outstanding record. On June 14, 1946, Boeing was authorized to further develop the design under the designation XB-52."*

In September 1947, the first of two prototypes of the B-47 Stratojet was rolled out in Seattle. That first test flight occurred on December 17, 1947, with weather giving considerable concern. The plane was to cross the Cascade range to Larson Air Force Base, near Moses Lake, Washington. The test pilot was Bob Robbins, the co-pilot Scott Osler. The plane was designed for a crew of three. Although no armament was carried on the first flight, the plane was designed to carry two .50-caliber machine guns in the tail. These could be fired manually from the cockpit by a gunner/bombardier or fired automatically by radar that locked onto any aircraft which might be pursuing the plane. Other traditional gun placements were deemed unnecessary due to the plane's great speed.

When the cloud cover finally cleared, the plane made its takeoff

---

*Richard L. Geer, "Air Force Systems Genesis: Top Down or Bottom Up" (Master's thesis, Georgetown University, Washington, D.C., 1968). Geer, the author's son, is principal engineer for Boeing's Experimental Development Programs.

The XB-47 (*Boeing P8813*)

without needing its eighteen JATO (Jet Assisted Take-Off) rockets, which could be fired from the sides of the plane to add thrust to the main jet engines. The bomber performed its flight tests beautifully, and when it touched down at Larson Field, Robbins said, "You have to fly it to appreciate it. She's beautiful!" Someone finally realized that this test flight took place on the forty-fourth anniversary of the Wright brothers' flight at Kitty Hawk.

There had been a great effort to get approval for the B-47 from those in the military who were still lukewarm to it. Bill Allen did his part by cozening General Wolfe, who had never before ridden in a jet, to stop at Larson Air Force Base briefly on his way east. Here the general was beguiled into "at least one short flight" in a B-47. The Air Force pilot at Larson, on this occasion, used those eighteen JATO rockets to get the plane into the air. It looked like a Fourth of July burst of fireworks soaring into the sky. Once the bomber was airborne, the pilot challenged Wolfe to take over the controls.

Several days later, George Schairer answered his home phone on a Saturday morning. The voice on the phone said, "I'm General Wolfe and I'm calling you because I've tried to get someone at Boeing to talk to. I've tried everyone from Bill Allen on down the chain of command and no one was at home. I want to know who

can I get in touch with to place an order for some B-47 planes."
Schairer gave Wolfe the number of Ed's cottage at Lake Meridian.

Ed later summarized the achievements of Boeing's first jets:
"The B-47's set spectacular records for their day, among them a
1949 flight in which the XB-47 covered 2,289 miles from Larson Air
Force Base in central Washington state to Andrews Air Force Base,
Maryland, in 3 hours 46 minutes, at an average speed of 607.8 miles
per hour. The last of the 1,390 B-47's built by Boeing Wichita was
delivered in October, 1956. Between them, Douglas and Lockheed
built an additional 667 Stratojets."*

With the success of the swept-wing, jet-powered B-47, a B-52
with propellers and straight wing no longer seemed the way to go,
although jet engines cut down a plane's range considerably since
they ate up fuel at an appalling rate. General LeMay was still having no compromise with range. "However," wrote Geer,

> by September of 1947, LeMay had cooled toward the B-52, the design was
> not meeting his range requirement, even with tremendously increased
> fuel capacity, and it was now out of hand in size and cost. In January
> 1948, the XB-52 had grown to a weight of 480,000 pounds and Wright
> Field was beginning to have strong doubts about the project.... Some-
> thing drastic had to be done, and the Weapons Board of the Air Force did
> it. They started to consider refueling to cut the XB-52 weight down to
> 300,000 pounds. On March 25 of that year, Secretary of the Air Force Stu-
> art Symington stated to the Senate Armed Services Committee that the
> new Air Force bombers, using "the most modern development of refuel-
> ing techniques ... can ... bomb any part of Russia, and return to Ameri-
> ca." Boeing was charged the next day to develop aerial refueling to make
> good the Secretary's statement. In April and May, the flying boom con-
> cept was developed by Mr. Cliff Leisy of Boeing and Captain Mack Elliot
> of the Air Force and approved by Lt. Col. Thomas Gerrity, chief of the
> B-50 program.

In October 1948 a team of Boeing engineers was at Dayton with
two proposals, one for the B-55 (a turboprop adaptation of the XB-
47, which never was put into production) and the one for B-52, with
possible jet engines.

Colonel "Pete" Warden looked at the latest attempt and, according to Vaughn Blumenthal, said, "that's nice. Thanks. But what
could you fellows do if you put a little more of the information you
have from the B-47 tests and information on the 460-40 with jet en-

*From Eleventh Wings Club Sight Lecture, New York City, May 15, 1974. According
to Bowers, *Boeing Aircraft since 1916*, p. 382, Boeing actually built 1,373 B-47s.

gines on the plane? We've got a fellow in the back room, a fellow from Germany, who is suggesting jet engines."

Warden had said he would be going back to the Pentagon the following week and wanted something to present. Schairer added, "He said he wanted something doggone soon!"

Warden's ultimatum came on a Thursday. The remarkable weekend that followed is the subject of a videotape made in 1979 by Lloyd Goodmanson of Boeing under the sponsorship of the American Institute of Aeronautics and Astronautics. Five of the six engineers who had been at Dayton "when the B-52 was finally designed" appeared on the video. (The sixth, Art Carlson, a weight and load specialist, had died.) In addition to Wells, they were Maynard Pennell, project engineer; George Schairer, staff engineer and chief aerodynamicist; "Bob" H. W. Withington, vice president/engineering, a wind tunnel specialist; and Blumenthal, director of preliminary design. Goodmanson, preliminary design manager, chaired the question-and-answer session on this videotape as the men reminisced.

The request from Warden had been sudden, but it was the culmination of years of frustration on both sides. "We never could seem to get anything the Air Force wanted," said Blumenthal. "The situation that led up to this weekend in Dayton was all in preparation for the coming of the big jet airplanes. But actually it represents a number of years of frustration on our part trying to put something together, something which could be better than what we had."

Schairer and Blumenthal called Ed in Wichita and told him, "We're in trouble. Get here as soon as you can." Ed arrived by early Friday morning. Warden told him to concentrate on speed, even at the expense of range. The six engineers went back to the Boeing Suite at the Van Cleve Hotel to roll up their sleeves. Wells laughed on the tape: "Calling it a 'suite' is a bit of a euphemism. It was two small rooms in which the intervening partition had been knocked out!"

On Friday evening Ed started to draw the new concept on Van Cleve Hotel stationery. Blumenthal and Withington began to make the mathematical estimates such as the ever-critical "lift-over-drag" formula. Carlson held everyone to weight restrictions. "I had my own handy-dandy means of estimating wing weight," said Pennell. "Actually the weight estimates we made that weekend came out to be almost identical with the weight of the finished plane."

Early Saturday morning Schairer began searching Dayton for a hobby shop that carried X-acto knives, balsa wood, doweling, glue, and a can of metallic spray paint. He started to turn Ed's drawings into an exquisite scale model of the plane. "George farmed out some of that work on making the model," recalled Ed. "Several of us were given jobs." The model was made on a 1-to-120 scale, not used in engineering, which Schairer defended on the basis of his equipment, "I guess I was using the only twelve-inch ruler available."

According to Blumenthal and Withington, the work was mostly just doubling the estimates they had in their briefcases from work on the B-55 and B-47, since the B-52 was going to be just twice the dimensions and weight of those planes. "We just doubled the wing area and the engines," said Withington. "We were either lucky or we were smart."

The group found a public stenographer to type their thirty-three-page document when they finished work. Then came the question of how to number it, a strict requirement of Boeing and Air Force regulations. They obviously couldn't get a number from the Seattle plant, which was closed over the weekend, so they "picked one out of a hat." Someone remembered the last document number he could recall having seen was in the late nine thousands, so they chose "a nice round number": 10,000. And that's the way the document has gone down in history, making D-10,000 famous at Boeing.

"Seattle was beside themselves with us choosing this number," said one of the engineers, "but we just said, 'Ed Wells signed it.'" The "ECW" initials were on every page of the document and on every one of Ed's original drawings. The document was submitted to Warden on Monday morning, and he proudly took it to the Pentagon.

"It was no miracle," said Schairer at the end of the videotape. "The story goes that we all met there and designed an airplane over the weekend, but that hardly fits the picture at all. We had all done our homework. And I hope this discussion would tell some of the fellows to get your homework done before a crisis situation. That weekend, fortunately, we came up with a winner." During Ed's presentation at the Wings Club in 1974, he said:

> In Boeing folklore there is a story of how the XB-52 was created in a room in the Van Cleve Hotel in Dayton, Ohio. Unlike some folklore, this story is literally true insofar as the first round or preliminary design was con-

cerned. Preliminary design layouts were made, a balsa model was carved, a weight statement was completed and preliminary performance was calculated. The only glitch occurred when the weight estimators in Seattle saw our weight statement for the first time and were horrified at our optimism. All was forgiven some time later, however, when the airplane was built within the preliminary estimate. Incidentally, George Schairer still has the balsa wood model, which bears a remarkable resemblance to the airplane finally built.

Wells elaborated the point in a letter to Richard Geer: "It is true that the first set of design data, including performance and weight estimates, preliminary specifications and scale model, was prepared in the Van Cleve for immediate subsequent presentation at Wright Field, but there was, of course, a substantial backlog of knowledge on both the XB-47 and the previous XB-52 designs to support the new model."

Geer summarizes what happened next:

In October Boeing was authorized by a directive of a board of Air Force officers to convert to a turbo-jet development. Boeing made official response in December with the 330,000 pound, 530 knot, 6,000 nautical mile range design conceived in Dayton. Yet, after the B-52 design was solidified, there was opposition. General LeMay wanted all-around armament and more range, being unwilling to accept a cruise speed reduction to 400 miles per hour to get it.... However, on January 1949, Headquarters, United States Air Force gave the green light to the XB-52 concept as we know it, presumably to General LeMay's eventual gratitude.

Eventually General LeMay did join the enthusiasts. Schairer recalled on the videotape that "the general put his arm around me and said, 'George, whatever you are doing to improve the B-47, stop doing it.' The general really wanted the B-52 to get into production with no delay."

Boeing received an order for two prototypes of the bomber, designated as the XB-52 and the YB-52. They were essentially the same plane, but by using the two designations the Air Force was able to allocate an extra $10 million in production funds to get the second plane built. The two planes cost an estimated $32 million, but after production got underway, B-52H models got down to $6 million apiece.

The XB-52 and the YB-52 first flew in 1952, and the first production machine, the B-52A, made its first flight August 5, 1954. The prototypes had tandem seating for pilot and copilot, but after LeMay insisted, with emphasis, that the plane be changed to a

The B52-H (*Boeing P26946*)

side-by-side seating arrangement in the cockpit, the production models from A through H changed to that design. On the videotape Ed remarked, "It was an argument between people who think if a plane flies like a fighter, it should look like a fighter, and those who think it should have a more roomy cockpit for bomber use."

In the B52-G and H models (the H was the last of the series), the tail gunner's space was moved to the aft upper deck behind the pilot. The tail guns were fired by remote control. Previously many of the tail gunners had been prone to violent air-sickness when the tail of the plane bagan to flutter in turbulent air.

The Air Force decided to use the B-52Hs in a low-altitude bombing strategy, with the planes slipping in under radar detection and tossing the bombs over the target. The B-52H plane also used fan-jet engines, which increased the propulsive air flow around the core engine.

Range was almost unlimited when the B-52s were refueled in flight by Boeing KC-135s. "Performance of the B-52 was outstand-

A B-52D being refueled by a KC-135 tanker (*Boeing K3813*)

ing," Ed said in his 1974 Wings Club speech. "Three of the big planes landed at March Air Force Base in January 1957, after an air refueled nonstop flight around the world, covering 24,325 miles from Castle Air Force Base, California, in 45 hours and 19 minutes at an average speed of 530 miles per hour. In January 1962, a B-52H flew nonstop 12,519 miles from Okinawa to Spain without refueling, breaking eleven distance and speed records."

There were 744 B-52s built. As of 1979, 344 were still in the Strategic Air Command inventory: 79 D models, 169 G models, and 96 H models. The engineers on the videotape expressed their pride that in the thirty years since the prototypes were built, the plane has remained "the backbone of the SAC inventory."

Between June 18, 1965, and August 15, 1973, B-52s flew 126,615 sorties in the Vietnam war. During that time, only seventeen B-52s were lost in combat.

A Boeing booklet entitled *Introduction to Engineering* uses the B-52 as an illustration of the demands of the profession:

To illustrate the amount of engineering necessary to produce a modern airplane, here are some statistics on the development of the Boeing B-52 Stratofortress, with its more than 100,000 individual parts:

By January 1, 1955, a total of approximately 34,500 separate drawings had to be made in this program.

These drawings, placed side by side, would cover the walls and ceilings of 110 five-room houses.

A total of 3,042,207 engineering man-hours was expended prior to the first flight, April 15, 1952. This is equal to one man working a five-day week for 1,462 years.

An additional 1,313,528 man-hours were expended by January 1, 1955 in flight testing the airplane.

When the first production model was rolled out, it alone had taken 3,827,850 man-hours of engineering work.

By January 1, 1955, a total of 11,529,544 man-hours of engineering work had been expended on the entire B-52 program, or the equivalent of one man working for 5,543 years.

In 1948, Ed was named vice president/engineering, with at least 3,000 engineers working under him, but promotion and recognition never changed him. One young engineer said, "Ed Wells would often walk up and down and look over the shoulders of us young engineers hunched over our drawing boards. He would often make a suggestion for an improvement of our design, then give us the credit for that innovation." Another said, "When you went to Wells's desk, no matter what he was doing, he always looked up to greet you with a warm smile."

Ed could also be tough. Another colleague said, "He goes about putting out fires quietly and with characteristic calm, and manages to keep people soothed, although he's no appeaser. There's nothing ivory tower or soft about his methods. You can leave Ed's office with your favorite project scrapped, but you'll leave happy."

At a memorial event after Ed's death, Thornton ("T.") Wilson, long-time chairman of the board at Boeing, summed up Ed's talents as a supervisor. "It was my good fortune to work for some great supervisors," he said, "but working for Ed was 'frosting on the cake.'... It was the character of the man, that if you had ever been associated with him you always felt he was your mentor.... He lost his patience so seldom that it was even more impressive because it was so seldom.... Ed Wells never encouraged me to do anything for the short-term company gain."

8

Jet Transports, Missiles, and the Moon

It was obvious by the late 1940s that jet power was going to make propeller driven aircraft obsolete. The problem was money—more acutely a problem of whose money. When Fred Collins of Boeing Sales told William Allen, "If we just had a jet transport prototype flying we could sell it," Allen shot back, "And whose money do you think you are spending?"

The British de Havilland Company had built a jet transport, calling it the Comet, and planned to demonstrate it at the Farnborough Air Show in September 1949. Allen dispatched Ed to England to see what was happening with jets. After the show, Ed took a brief trip with the Boeing European representative, Kenneth Luplow, to Belgium, France, Switzerland, and Germany. Upon his return, Ed told Allen, "We will have to get a quick start on a prototype to compete with the Comet, and it will have to be a superior plane to sell to Europe. Their dollar credits are limited."*

But there was still no financing in sight. When it finally came into being, the Boeing commercial transport as a jet plane would be the Boeing 707, closely related to the Air Force KC-135 tanker/C-135 transport, which was a successor to a proposed improvement over the Air Force KC-97.

The history of this jet transport evolution is well told by Richard Geer:

In June of 1946 the Boeing preliminary design section started a systematic design study of turbojet commercial transports. The job was assigned

---

*Ed described his trip to Farnborough in his Eleventh Wings Club Sight Lecture, New York City, May 15, 1974.

124

to two men: Robert Hage, former aerodynamicist chief at Wright Field, who had lead responsibility, and Richard Fitzsimmons as a helper. In 1949 Hage's study had indicated that a jet transport was feasible, but none of his designs appeared exactly right.

In October 1949, one year after the creation of the B-52 concept, Wells and Schairer were once more in Dayton over a weekend. They were examining wind tunnel results of an improved B-52 wing with John Alexander, a Boeing aerodynamicist, and fell to discussing jet transport design. They designed and sketched out, on the spot, a low-wing transport using essentially the B-52 wing design, with jet engines in separate pods on swept-back wings and a tricycle gear retracting into the body. The three returned to Seattle and passed the new design to the company's preliminary design section.

In November 1950, the Air Force Senior Officers' Board came to Seattle to discuss B-52 production proposals. Boeing presented a proposal for a turboprop KC-97 tanker/transport but aroused no interest. Major General Carl Brandt suggested putting jets on it to get significant improvement. With such encouragement, Boeing started immediately on such a design—a KC-97 with modest (25 degree) sweep-back and turbojet power.*

Boeing's hopes were raised when, in January 1951, a request was received from Wright Field concerning the KC-97 with turbojet engines. The company stepped up work on the modified design, but around the middle of August the Air Force notified Boeing it had decided against the KC-97 turbojet. Boeing made an attempt to reverse this decision, but without success.

For its next attempt, Boeing decided to make a fresh start. "This time," wrote Geer, "there was no attempt to retain existing tooling or design features. The new design was given the designation 'Model 707.' By early 1952 the 707 design, similar in most respects to the final concept, but with dual podded engines, looked sufficiently appealing to gamble on."

The preliminary studies had been attempts to improve the Model 367 (in production for the Air Force as the C-97 Stratofreighter). The basic Model 367 did eventually go through its eightieth change. Its jet-powered variants could no longer be recognized as the C-97 Stratofreighter, although the designation Model 367 was retained. It was called the 367-80, and this designation was kept as a means of maintaining company secrecy over the project until it was completed. In company circles, it was always referred to as the Dash-Eighty. It differed from the military bombers in that it was a

*Richard Geer, "Air Force Systems Genesis: Top Down or Bottom Up" (Master's thesis, Georgetown University, Washington, D.C., 1968).

The Dash-Eighty roll-out (*Boeing P14306*)

low-wing, tricycle-gear design with four individually podded engines.

When Ed brought the 707 in to Allen's office for approval, Allen liked the looks of it, and he realized that Ed was also extremely pleased with the design. Allen took the next step, giving Ed and four other key staff members a lengthy questionnaire on the feasibility of funding a prototype. According to Geer,

> The answers came in, on April 21, all favorable. The next day the board of directors voted $15,000,000 to build the prototype as a gamble.
>
> The 707 system concept...was established in July. The dual pod engines had been scrapped in favor of four separate pods. George Schairer,

now chief of technical staff, was heard to observe that it was not too different from the Sunday afternoon sketches made in October 1949 in Dayton.

Lloyd Goodmanson, project engineer for the prototype, is quoted in *Boeing Magazine,* April 1955, that "the early rollout of the prototype, appreciably months ahead of schedule—was in itself a demonstration of the plane's basic simplicity. The extreme rapidity with which functional tests were accomplished was another demonstration of the same thing."

The $15 million was "a substantial part of the company's net worth," Ed recalled in his 1974 Wings Club lecture, "and would be equivalent to nearly $100 million today." John Yeasting, Boeing's finance officer, had brought in a report of earnings for 1951 of $7 million and predicted the earnings should double for Boeing for the following year.

The Dash-Eighty was rolled from the Renton factory on May 15, 1954, and made its first flight on July 15. It was the thirty-eighth anniversary of Boeing's founding, and Ed recalled that William E. Boeing "watched his wife christen the aircraft which ushered in the jet transport age for America. Although no longer associated with the company, he was able to view the fruits of his pioneering efforts which had begun four decades earlier."

The first order for a commercial jet was received from Pan American World Airways in October 1955, and the plane was put in service on Pan Am's transatlantic route on October 26, 1958. (Charles Lindbergh's association with Pan Am was a plus for Boeing; the famed aviator had come to Seattle to meet Ed during production of the B-17, and Ed had maintained the acquaintance with his boyhood hero.) The Dash-Eighty prototype is now owned by the Smithsonian Institution and is temporarily on loan to the Museum of Flight in Seattle.

George Martin, Ed's longtime associate, said:

Ed made many of the sales presentations of the new jets to the airlines. Ed was very prescient in his relations with Boeing customers and had the great ability to determine the customers' requirements and what design features would satisfy those requirements.

In the first sales contest for the commercial jet business, Pan American World Airways purchased twenty-five Douglas DC-8's and Boeing received an order for only twenty 707 planes. This was a shock to Boeing, particularly so, because Boeing had a prototype flying and could offer earlier deliveries. However, Douglas had selected a fuselage-diameter three inches greater than the Boeing 707 diameter and the DC-8 had a somewhat larger wing with greater span.

United Air Lines was the next company ready to make a decision. Douglas had built up a fuselage mock-up which demonstrated the difference in interior spaciousness resulting from their 3-inch greater diameter fuselage. United placed an order for 30 DC-8 transports. Now, Boeing was deeply concerned.

American Airlines was now prepared to select an airplane for its jet fleet. Ed Wells travelled to Oklahoma City to confer with American management. At five o'clock in the morning on a cold November day, I received a long-distance call from Ed. It went something like this: "George, it's not going very well down here. We're not going to interest American with our present fuselage diameter. Now I have been doing some sketching on a three-view drawing. I think we can fair in a larger diameter midsection fuselage to the present nose and tail section. Here is what I want you to do today. Determine what increased diameter body can be accommodated—then go see Bob Regan, head of manufacturing, and determine that he can handle the change. Then go over to Bill Allen and advise him on what we are planning to do and get his approval to proceed. Call me back no later than four o'clock this afternoon."

I got the best loftsman in the company and went to work. Yes, we could fair in a bigger diameter fuselage to the tail and nose section. While we were making the change, it seemed wise to select a diameter slightly greater than the DC-8. We chose an increase of 4½ inches and set the maximum fuselage diameter exactly at shoulder height. Then back to Bob Regan: he felt his fuselage could be revised to accommodate the 4½-inch increase. On to Bill Allen: after listening to the proposition and after considerable thought, Bill responded, "I don't like it, but if that is what it takes to sell American, you call Ed and tell him I concur on the change."

Just before 4 P.M. I called Ed and told him the results of the day's activity and the fuselage diameter. Ed responded, "Thank you, George, I think we have just sold some airplanes." Several days later American announced they had contracted for thirty 707 Boeing jet transports.

Later, Pan American Airways was pleased to accept the increased diameter fuselage on their initial order of twenty 707's. Thus, all 707's were built to this larger diameter and this same size has been used for the 727, 737 and 757 series airplanes.

During the same period, the Air Force was debating the military usefulness of jet tankers. The B-52 had been controversial, in part because of refueling problems, and it had not been ordered into production until August 1952, delaying the opportunity to evaluate the plane in action. According to Geer:

> The Strategic Air Command finally decided on the 19th of November, 1953, that it wanted the Boeing tanker with J-57 engines.... The Command's decision reached Boeing in the spring of 1954 as a requirement

for jet tankers, period. Allen authorized spending company funds to start engineering and tooling work for a production airplane, in order to meet an October 1956 delivery date.

The Air Force was still far from agreed upon a tanker decision. The contenders included turboprop tankers and converted B-36's and B-47's. While the discussion was going on, the 707 was rolled out as a dual purpose airplane-prototype for the hoped-for commercial and tanker versions. . . . Despite the fact that the Boeing airplane was at least two years ahead of any alternate jet tanker design, the competition was still very much in the picture. The Air Force had by now decided it would buy jet-powered aircraft, but could not settle on the 707, the newly announced DC-8, the giant turboprop Douglas C-132 now in the second year of Air Force sponsored development, a new Lockheed design or a Wright Air Development Center "Design 1018."

August 5, 1954, the Air Force announced it would buy an interim quantity of 29 jet tankers from Boeing pending the results of a forthcoming competition to decide on a tanker design for quantity production.

In September 1954, the Air Force realized that the incorporation of both an interim and a competition tanker from Douglas and Lockheed into the Strategic Air Command inventory made very little sense and the idea was dropped.

The official history has it: "The Air Force's decision to buy the Boeing airplane instead of the technical winner of the competition was a calculated risk that paid off—the record shows that the decision was a wise one. The Air Force had accepted approximately 100 jet tankers from Boeing before Boeing's nearest competitor had flown its jet transport for the first time."

The Air Force called these transport/tankers the KC-135s. They could be fitted with flying-boom nozzles to make possible the transfer of fuel to the B-52 in the air. Later the booms were adapted to permit "probe and drogue" refueling from the boom. At last General LeMay would have his B-52s with "unlimited range."

"The main thing I remember," LeMay said, "is Ed's attention to what we peons who flew the airplane wanted and what's more, producing it."

The grand total for the KC/C-135 Stratotanker series was 820 aircraft, including 732 jet tankers and forty-five C-135 cargo versions.

The company-funded prototype was a calculated risk that eventually paid off. "Two [later] incidents furnished rather spectacular evidence of the value of having a prototype," Goodmanson told *Boeing Magazine* in an article published in April 1955. "In the first, secondary loads imposed by deflection caused a landing gear attachment to give way under unusually severe stress during a taxiing test. In the second incident, brakes failed on landing. Because

The KC-135 tanker equipped with a Boeing-developed refueling boom
(*Boeing P23839*)

these experiences occurred during prototype tests, need for costly
production model adjustments was forestalled."

That mishap with the landing gear had occurred, much to Ed's
chagrin, on May 21, 1954, late in the afternoon while the Boeing test
pilot, Tex Johnston, was making a taxi test. The giant plane lurched
over on the runway as the left landing gear collapsed. Martin and
Pennell rushed out to view the damage, and Allen was wired the
news in Wichita. When Allen returned to Seattle, Ed confessed to
him that the trouble seemed to be poor design and an untested
piece of steel. He expected to be reprimanded, possibly demoted,
since the 707 project was so critical to Boeing's future. Allen said
only, "We don't like mistakes, but the important thing is to learn
from them."

Allen may have remembered that two of the British jet-powered
Comets had fallen apart in the air from "metal fatigue." Boeing
joined forces with other members of the Aircraft Industries Association to work for better specification standards for aircraft steel.

The next year, Johnston terrified Bill Allen and Ed by doing two slow barrel rolls in the prototype 707, over the heads of a quarter million spectators at the Seattle Gold Cup hydroplane races. It was certainly an unscheduled entertainment, but no one doubted the strength of the plane after that.

The quick responses to customers' needs that characterized the designs of the B-52 and original 707 also were factors in other planes in the 707 series. George Martin recalled that after the enlargement of the 707 cabin,

once again, Boeing was locked in competition with Douglas. Now it was for business with our European customers for jet transports for the transatlantic routes. Our slightly smaller 707 was marginal on range and fuel capacity for these routes. In preliminary design we had been experimenting with relatively small changes in the airplane configuration which resulted in only small improvements.

Finally . . . Ed Wells came to my office and said he felt we were losing the contest with our smaller airplane. What was needed was major change to increase the airplane's capability. More span, more wing area, more fuel capacity. Further, the "Boss" was ready to support a major change. Wells emphasized that time was of the essence.

The preliminary design room went into high gear. Between Thursday afternoon and Sunday noon, a new configuration was drawn up. The wing span was increased by adding five feet to the root of each wing, effectively moving all jet motors five feet further out from the fuselage. This change increased both the wing area and fuel capacity. The fuselage was lengthened, the tail surfaces were increased in size and a larger jet engine (the J-75) was selected. On Sunday evening, armed with the new proposal and supported by a twenty-five page document outlining the new plane's capability, three teams of Boeing salesmen flew off to Europe.

The new model was called the 707 Intercontinental. In a short time Boeing won orders for this new configuration from BOAC, Air France, Lufthansa and Sabena airlines.

As the jet transport market grew, there developed a need for a jet plane well suited for intermediate-length flights. Convair had brought out their Model 880 and were at work on their Model 990 for the intermediate-range market.

At Boeing Ed Wells thought the market niche could be well filled by a lightened up version of the 707. The span and wing area were kept the same, but the wing weight was reduced and the fuselage was somewhat shortened. A speed-glove was added to the inner wing leading edge, resulting in a wing with a higher critical speed. This variation of the 707 series was given the model number of 720. Wells then influenced Boeing to price their initial offering so attractively that United and other airlines placed orders for this model transport.

Intercontinental version of the 707 (*Boeing P29141*)

For all practical purposes, the Boeing 720 won the market niche and Convair was eliminated as a viable contender for the jet transport market. I know from my association with Ed that these three decisions contributed greatly to the success of the 707 family of airplanes.

George Schairer, who probably worked more closely with Ed than anyone else at Boeing, believed that "Ed was at the center of most of the major product decisions at Boeing." Schairer praised Ed not only for his attention to customers but also for the strength of character to acknowledge flaws in a design that had already been built.

All too often a designer has great difficulty acknowledging defects in his latest design, let alone selling management upon an immediate program to correct such deficiencies. Ed Wells was a master at getting Boeing people to look for and see inadequacies and problems in their latest brain children. He was then a master at getting Boeing to initiate and pay for or sell a correction or improvement program.

Interestingly, Ed almost never spoke up about his questions and views. He waited for others to initiate such conversations. Many were the design meetings I have been in where Ed sat by himself and made copious notes, but volunteered nothing until he was asked to speak up. This was usually after nearly all others in the group had sounded off in all sorts of directions and it was up to Ed to show and suggest a course of action which all could agree to.

I remember many design review meetings involving six to sixty people where the objective of the meeting was to define the principal physical characteristics of a possible product such as the SST, so as to most nearly meet a customer's stated desires. Most of us in such meetings thought of our actions as being aimed at "optimization" of a design. By "optimization" we meant we were comparing several different workable designs to find out which one most nearly met a customer's desires. Ed would sometimes point out that our latest sketch of a possible product contained one or more of what he called "fatal defects." To Ed a "fatal defect" in a design included such items as excessive take-off noise, an unacceptable sonic boom, an inability to operate from existing airports or existing runways, an inability to meet federal safety regulations, etc. Ed would subtly point out that we had to get rid of all "fatal defects" before we could "optimize." Ed Wells was at his best at "fixing what was wrong."*

In 1951, still only forty, Wells was elected to the Board of Directors of Boeing. That same year, the family moved from Cascadia Avenue across Lake Washington to a lakefront home near the enclave of Beaux Arts, a former artists' colony surrounded by the city limits of Bellevue. The family had long since outgrown Ed's first homemade boat and had been converted to more ambitious boats by Evelyn and Claire Egtvedt, who invited Ed and Dorothy to join them on their large sailing yacht for a weekend cruise on Puget Sound. "It was so great to be on the water away from the ringing of telephones day and night, with no letters to be answered, no telegrams to read, no questions or problems to be solved," Ed said. In 1949, Ed found what he wanted: a thirty-four-foot second-hand cabin cruiser named *Whimsy*. He had arranged for it to be moored at the Seattle Yacht Club marina near the University of Washington, where, in what little spare time he could hoard, he might polish and paint and caulk and varnish and buff.

The family got away for some weekends on the water, but not as many as Ed would have liked. The yacht club was several miles from their home, and the children were busy with their own projects. Laurie Jo, an enthusiastic artist, produced her own four-to-

*Letter from George Schairer to the author.

ten-page booklets for sale to the neighborhood children, priced at forty cents apiece. One booklet which is still in the family contains over one hundred names suggested by Laurie Jo as appropriate for pet animals. She classified the names as being appropriate for dogs, cats, monkeys, raccoons, squirrels, snakes, birds, and gold-fish. Edward Elliott's pride was his new Lionel "O" gauge train, which could spin around on a track parallel with his father's train tracks in the basement. He also liked planes and with his allowance bought balsa models, some of them powered by twisted rubber bands.

The new home meant that the *Whimsy* could be moored at the family dock, cutting down on travel time to and from the yacht club. On clear days the house looked out upon the majesty of snow-capped Mt. Rainier down the lake to the south. Wild ducks and Canada geese made themselves at home on the grass and among the shrubs and under the great native madrona trees. A horse was bought for Laurie Jo, and a beautiful collie dog became a new family member. The children got a metal canoe for paddling on the lake, and in 1954 Ed and Dorothy purchased another boat, the *Whimsy II*, a shiny new thirty-seven-foot Chris-Craft cruiser that slept six.

Ed still had limited time to enjoy the new home and boat. In 1954 he served on the Industry Advisory Board of the Arnold Engineer-ing Development Center of the Air Research and Development Command in Tullahoma, Tennessee. The board's job was "to re-view policy matters pertaining to the design, construction and op-eration of the Center." That same year he met with thirty-three oth-er leading aircraft industry executives at Kirtland Air Force Base, New Mexico, for a one-day seminar "on utilization of aircraft in the nuclear weapons field." This was followed up by a two-day semi-nar a year later. He was also appointed to act as a member of an Air Force Advisory Committee, whose duties were defined in a news release as "assisting in the development of ways of further improv-ing cooperation and collaboration between Air Materiel and Air Re-search and Development."

One of Ed's extracurricular responsibilities was undertaken out of sheer sentimentality. When he was asked to become a member of the Board of Directors for the Northwestern Mutual Life Insur-ance Company of Milwaukee, Wisconsin, he did not have the heart to turn them down. His beloved uncle, Hans Roan, had been Gen-eral Agent for the Northwestern for the state of Idaho, and had been immensely proud of the connection. Roan bought Ed his first modest life insurance policy. In 1961 the insurance company decid-

Artist's rendering of Wells at the controls of his second cabin cruiser, the *Whimsy II*, and (above) on a cruise with friends, aboard the *Whimsy* (Warren McCallister, artist)

ed it would like to use Wells's name and reputation in nationwide advertising. The company arranged for the famous portrait photographer Yousuf Karsh to go to Seattle to take photographs of Ed. These would appear in *Life, Time,* and other large-circulation magazines. The full-page ad mentioned that Ed had purchased his first policy at age nineteen. The advertisement included this advice from Ed: "The moral is here for all to see. The future doesn't just happen . . . it starts the day you plan for it." Ed was embarrassed by the publicity, but was persuaded it would be "good advertising for Boeing." Only Ed's immediate family knew about the ad, providing a welcome surprise to the other relatives when they opened their magazines that month.

Ed was president of the Institute of Aeronautical Sciences for the year 1958–59, and he and Dorothy flew to Madrid for the group's annual meeting. Afterwards they spent two weeks touring Europe by car. Also in 1958 he vacated his post as vice president/ engineering of Boeing to assume the position of vice president/ general manager of Boeing's newly formed Systems Management Office, which would encompass the missile and space programs.

Boeing had become interested in getting into the missile business soon after the end of World War II. In 1945 the Ground-to-Air-Pilotless-Aircraft (GAPA) project got started. After dozens of the missiles had been built, a controversy between the Air Force and the Army caused the cancellation of the Air Force contract with Boeing, because this was a short-range missile (less than 100 miles) and the Army claimed jurisdiction. Because of this decision, the Air Force suggested that Boeing cooperate with the University of Michigan in developing a longer-range missile. Thus Boeing received a contract in January 1951 to develop the supersonic Bomarc, a defense weapon that could destroy enemy planes or airborne missiles at distances of up to 400 miles. December 1957 saw the roll-out of the first production model, and production ended in the middle of 1962. Bomarc missiles were operational in both the United States Air Defense Command and the Canadian Air Force.

In a prophetic article published in the *Boeing Magazine* in July 1951, Ed had predicted that "in the fighter plane field especially, we will watch the plane and missile becoming more nearly the same. The missile will be smaller than the airplane and take along no 'missile' to fire at the enemy, it being the missile. The fighter will take along a 'missile' to fire and perhaps a man on board. The man will go along for the ride, as his flight will be essentially electronically controlled. His prime duties will be to see that everything goes all right and that the fighter gets back to base. The systems of the two aircraft will be very comparable."

In 1958, the Minuteman missile program was entrusted to Boeing. The company would be responsible for the assembly, test, installation, launch control, and ground support system for this intercontinental ballistic missile. Wells chose T. Wilson, previously project manager on the B-52, to be proposal and program manager. Wilson was a brilliant young engineer who had been chosen as a Sloan Fellow and given a year's leave of absence from Boeing to pursue study in industrial management at Massachusetts Institute of Technology.

Setting a record for design-development-production-delivery of a major Air Force weapon system, the first two Minuteman missile wings became operational in October 1962, at Malstrom Air Force Base, Montana, only four years after the program was set in motion. According to Ed in his speech before the Wings Club,

> the planned 1000 Minuteman missiles were operational with six wings by early 1967. Delivery of all wings was made on or ahead of schedule. The company has continued as the major associate contractor on the Minuteman program as Minuteman II and Minuteman III missiles have been developed to replace the earlier missiles, and the launch complexes have been "hardened" to resist nuclear blast effects.

Boeing also produced the Air Force's Short Range Attack Missile (SRAM), a supersonic air-to-ground missile carried by the B-52 and FB-111 bombers of the Strategic Air Command. The missiles were very versatile. They were armed with nuclear warheads and could attack defense installations or penetrate to primary targets. And they could be launched at subsonic or supersonic speeds, from high or low altitude, and could hit targets ahead of their launching aircraft or turn in flight to strike targets ahead of or behind the aircraft.

In August 1959 the Boeing Aerospace Division was formed by a consolidation of Boeing's Seattle Division, its Pilotless Aircraft Division, and its Systems Management Division of which Wells had been vice president and general manager. At this consolidation, Wells was promoted to a newly created post, corporate vice president/engineering, where his main role was to provide policy guidance. His broader role made it possible to take a break from day-to-day engineering responsibilities, and Ed and Dorothy decided to sell their boat and, with the money, take the children for a six-week tour of Europe. The family had been able to have so few vacations

Test firing of the Minuteman missile, 1961 (*Boeing 2B3790*)

The Lunar Orbiter (*Boeing P38930*)

together, and this seemed like the year to take the big one. Ed used to grin and repeat the old saying of boat owners, "The happiest day of a man's life is when he buys his boat, and the second happiest is the day he sells it."

In November of that year, Boeing became involved with the famous Dyna-Soar program for the Air Force. This was conceived as a manned boost-glide vehicle that could operate in or out of earth's atmosphere. The program would require extensive research into new materials, structures, and guidance technology never used before. The re-entry heat was one of the critical problems. Unfortu-

The Lunar Roving Vehicle (*Boeing P47590*)

nately for Boeing, the Dyna-Soar project was canceled in midstream in December 1963, necessitating a layoff of several thousand Boeing employees.

When Boeing lost the Dyna-Soar program, they were heartened by immediately picking up a contract from the National Aeronautics and Space Administration (NASA) for the Lunar Orbiter spacecraft, which, in Ed's words, "turned out to be one of the most successful programs of all time." The contract asked for the building of eight vehicles: three for ground tests and five for flight. Boeing achieved a remarkable record. The first flight vehicle, the *Orbiter*, was launched for the moon on August 10, 1966, just over twenty-eight months after the contract was inked. It was to circle the moon to take hundreds of pictures of the moon's surface, so that landing sites could be picked out for the manned Apollo mission. Since the first three flights gave the scientists enough information to select Apollo program sites, the final flight vehicles were used for other missions.

In December 1961, NASA picked Boeing as the contractor to build the first stage of the giant Saturn booster, which would mea-

The 747 rollout in Everett, September 30, 1968 (*Boeing P43710*)

sure 138 feet high and 33 feet in diameter, and weigh over 5 million pounds when loaded for launching. This first stage would generate the equivalent of 180 million horsepower. This remarkable engineering effort by Boeing would produce the only major launch system never to experience an in-flight failure.

Saturn V was launched in its first successful flight on November 9, 1967, from Cape Kennedy, and less than two years later—July 1969—men landed on the moon. Six Saturn boosters led to manned lunar landings, and in May 1973 Saturn V launched *Skylab* into orbit as its last scheduled flight.

In April 1965, Boeing received a contract from the Air Force Space and Missile Systems Office in Los Angeles to design and build an upper-stage vehicle called Burner II to place small and medium payloads in orbit. Richard Geer was personally involved with this program and describes it in his thesis:

> Ling-Temco-Vought and The Boeing Company were selected in July [1964] to define their concepts in terms of design, cost and performance. After a keen competition lasting through November, Boeing was selected and commenced work on a fixed price development and initial production contract in April 1965. . . .
>
> The Boeing concept stressed simplicity, incorporation of off-the-shelf equipment and ease of production, test and launch assembly/maintenance. The aerodynamics, including control moments and acoustic vibration considerations, were so obviously good that no model testing was necessary. . . .
>
> On 29 June 1967, the Burner II placed two satellites, one Army and one Navy, into 2100 nautical circular orbits with a special Burner II "payload dispenser" providing high altitude orbital injection capability. It was the third Burner II launch.

Burner II had twenty-four launches, twenty-three of which were successful. The failed launch was judged to be not the fault of the Burner II itself.

In October 1969, NASA chose Boeing to design and build the vehicle to move astronauts over the surface of the moon. The Lunar Roving Vehicle (LRV) traveled at an average speed of 8 mph on a relatively level surface, and the LRV on *Apollo 17* managed more than 11 mph traveling down a moon mountain. In his speech to the Wings Club, Ed said that the Rovers used on *Apollo 15, 16,* and *17* tripled the amount of information the astronauts could collect because of their LRV mode of locomotion.

Boeing also was responsible for the Mariner Venus-Mercury probe built under the direction of NASA's Jet Propulsion Laboratory.

In addition, Boeing was dominating commercial aviation during this period. The company announced the go-ahead decision for the 727 trijet in December 1960. The initial flight took place February 9, 1963, and on December 24 the Federal Aviation Administration certificated the type for commercial production.

Plans for the world's largest commercial airplane, the 747, were announced in early 1966, and in April Pan American announced a purchase of twenty-five 747s. In the next few months, a total of $1.8 billion in airline orders for the superjets was received—one of the largest pre-production orders in commercial airplane history. In his speech to the New York Wings Club, Ed summed up Boeing's achievement. "Since that day in 1958 when the 707 ushered in the jet transport age, Boeing has delivered nearly 2,500 jet aircraft to the world's airlines—approximately half of all the commercial jet transports in operation throughout the world." He also reminded listeners that Boeing's reputation for financial and political conservatism "reflects part of the company's many-faceted personality, but only part. The company has had another face which the public generally does not recognize. It's an innovative and risk-taking corporate visage, marked with many successes and some failures. To an extent, it is a mirror image of the turbulent times of the past half century."

Perhaps the greatest disappointment for Boeing was the cancellation of the Supersonic Transport (SST) project, in which, as Ed pointed out, "many engineering lifetimes had been invested."

9

Disappointments and a Look into the Future

In 1951, Ed wrote an article for the July issue of *Boeing Magazine*, marking the thirty-fifth anniversary of the founding of the company. Already, he was deeply interested in the potentials and problems of supersonic flight, and he had a cogent grasp of the financial and technical factors involved.

> Because military economy is based upon maximum speed and range, while commercial economy is based on low operating costs, planes in the two fields may grow farther apart. This separation of fields may diminish, however, when the turbo-jet plane is accepted as standard transportation in commercial aviation.
>
> What about the commercial plane of the future?... it need not face a sonic barrier so long as it is economical to travel at supersonic speeds. This type of economy will come only with increased efficiency of engines and airplanes and new traffic control plans.
>
> Any great increase in speed does bring many technical problems, but they can be solved as the need arises. One of the main questions is the technical problem of physiology that confronts us with flight at extreme altitudes. High speed, of course, can mean going up to altitudes where pressure failures result in total disaster. With man's blood boiling at 60,000 feet, one can readily see the need for failure-proof systems, or developments to permit high-speed flight at moderately high altitudes.

Boeing's first supersonic manned airplane was the TFX (tactical fighter experimental) contract, which culminated in the building of the F-111 fighter plane for the Air Force, but not by Boeing. The company was aced out in a very controversial decision.

This project began in July 1960 when the Wright Air Development Center sent out requests for proposals on a variable swept-wing tactical fighter. Boeing had already been working for a year on ideas along the lines of this requested proposal, so they assumed they might be slightly ahead of the game.

Geer provides the background for the TFX saga:

> The variable-sweep wing portion of the F-111 system concept came from a chance juxtaposition of the Tactical Air Command and NASA facilities at Langley Air Force Base, Virginia. The Tactical Air Command had a requirement for an aircraft that could loiter long, fly long distance unrefueled and yet have supersonic low altitude capability. General Frank Everest, then commander at Langley, discussed the problem with the noted aerodynamicist, John Stack, of NASA. Stack suggested the swing-wing concept and started a team . . . to work on the idea. The team came up with an outboard pivot design. . . . The Langley researchers advised The Boeing Company (who immediately started work) and the Navy, who contracted with North American and Douglas Aircraft to investigate feasibility. By late 1959, the Tactical Air Command had drawn up a formal requirements statement with NASA assistance.
>
> The statement met with less than enthusiastic response from Headquarters, United States Air Force and the Air Development Command, which had already proved the concept unfeasible with the X-5 research aircraft (which was essentially an adaptation of the World War II Messerschmidt design). Under the powerful influence of Stack's prestige, the Air Staff approved the request in February 1960, which defined the Air Force version of the TFX. Variable sweep was not explicitly called for, but it was an obvious necessity. Other features of the Air Force aircraft included a fineness ratio of 12 and an overall length of 80 feet for maximum range and speed.
>
> It was at approximately this same time that the Navy also asked for a long-range airborne carrier defense system. They believed they needed an airplane with swing-wing, two-place seating, but with a length limited to 55 feet (a limit of length so that the plane could be accommodated by the elevator space on any carrier). This plane was needed to implement use of a new air-to-air missile and would need to have, therefore, supersonic dash capability.

There was a change in administration in Washington and a replacement, naturally, of all cabinet officers. Robert McNamara was appointed as Secretary of Defense to replace Thomas Gates. When he got into office, McNamara discovered that the Navy and Air Force were each asking for a swing-wing airplane, and he wanted to save the taxpayer's money by making it the same plane. "Commonality" was one of his pet words, from his experience, apparently, in manufacturing automobiles. He soon learned that his decision was unpopular, recalling according to Geer's thesis that "the majority of experts in the Navy and Air Force said it couldn't be done. As late as the 22nd of August 1961, it was reported to me by both services that . . . it was not technically feasible."

Geer describes the design that resulted:

> The compromise airplane was 63 feet long, with about double the wave drag and reduced range at both high and low altitudes, compared to the Air Force requirements. On the other hand, the increase in length over Navy requirements restricted it to carriers of the Midway class and larger, and these larger attack carriers could have accommodated a still larger airplane. On September 1, 1961, after reviewing the Navy and Air Force objections to the TFX concept, McNamara ordered it done.

The competition to build the controversial TFX was then narrowed, at last, to a combined General Dynamics–Grumman proposal versus a Boeing proposal. McNamara again stepped into the picture personally, calling for reappraisal every time the technical selection seemed to be leaning towards Boeing. When this had occurred on several occasions, the U.S. Senate began to take notice. The military chiefs announced that the Boeing proposal was technically better and cost less. But McNamara announced that the contract would be awarded to General Dynamics. "Boeing simply did not meet the fundamental requirement of minimum divergence from a common design," he said, "and no amount of peripheral technical argument should be permitted to obscure this central and crucial fact." McNamara also argued that Boeing had underestimated the costs of the titanium and thrust reversers in its proposal.*

The Senate established the McClellan Committee in the spring of 1963 to investigate the matter. Geer wrote that the committee wanted to know if it was rational for "commonality to be central" or "technical arguments to become peripheral" where the national defense was concerned. Bill Allen felt that the Boeing Company should not get involved and did not want to appear as a witness before the Senate committee. But Ed, by this time a senior vice president of Boeing, finally persuaded him that they should answer the summons, at least to clear the engineering department in the eyes of the public and the military. Ed went to Washington.

McNamara had contended that commonality could cut a substantial amount from the total cost of $6.5 billion. Senator McClellan pursued the point with Ed, asking if such savings were likely given

---

*U.S. Congress, Senate, Committee on Government Operations, *TFX Contract Investigations* (88th Cong., 1st sess., 1963), pt. 2, p. 382.

that only 200 of the 1,700 aircraft were for the Navy. McClellan did not think so, and Ed agreed, "unless someone gets very careless."

Ed defended Boeing's method of estimating costs, and reviewed his own experiences with "commonality":

> I am old enough to have been a designer on a highly successful common design produced by my company for both Air Corps and Navy use [the P-12 and F-4B series of fighters], but I'm young enough to remember that the idea worked well then and why it worked. Because it worked then and is not a new concept by any means, I am confident that it can be made to work again. But here I must draw an important distinction. It would not have worked then if we or the military services had accepted the philosophy that it is necessary to sacrifice performance in any significant degree to achieve some arbitrarily selected measure of merit such as number of identical parts. To have accepted this philosophy then would have presented our potential enemies with a gift of military superiority.
>
> Accepting it today would offer them the same gift. The concept that at any point in calendar time we can afford to be ultraconservative in such a way as to fail to obtain readily available military superiority is inconceivable to me, as I believe it must be to any dedicated professional military officer. If this had been our philosophy, we would have entered World War II prepared only to produce B-18's rather than B-17's; B-29's would have been unpressurized and would have been armed with hand-held machine guns. B-47's would have been built without performance superiority provided by the swept-back wing; B-52's would have been built with turboprop engines of inferior performance; and both B-47's and B-52's would still be refueled with propeller-driven tankers.
>
> This, then, is the basic issue which must be joined. When large steps can clearly be taken in military capability, will the enemy permit us the luxury of taking a smaller step, however skillfully rationalized?
>
> If the price of a superior system were higher, certainly a weighing of cost versus result would be in order. However, in the TFX competition the fixed price quoted by Boeing is clearly lower and is backed up by firm incentive, bonus and penalty provisions.
>
> Again, as a professional engineer, I hope that I can continue to assume that superior weapons are important to our national security. If our philosophy should ever be "marginally acceptable is good enough," we are in a sorry predicament indeed.
>
> It is my earnest hope that this Committee can clearly establish a weakness of such a philosophy, and that in its place a philosophy of competitive superiority can be re-established.

Senator Henry Jackson of Washington state was a member of the McClellan Committee, and was highly concerned (even angry) when he heard of the award of the TFX to General Dynamics. He was on his way to Hawaii, but told Allen he'd get in touch with Mc-

Clellan. For a time it seemed there might be a reversal of the verdict on the award. In fact, Allen was put on the spot by the committee, by being asked if he favored a reversal with Boeing getting the contract, or a decision to have each competitor build a plane, at which time a choice could be rendered. Nothing came of the hearings as far as the TFX was concerned.

Apparently, Jackson could do nothing. The McClellan Committee did not override McNamara's decision to give the contract to General Dynamics, despite the unanimous recommendation of a Pentagon Source Selection Board that it go to Boeing.

The committee concluded in its final report that "top presidential appointees in the Department of Defense during the McNamara era overrode expert advice to impose personal judgment on complex matters beyond their expertise."

More glaring weaknesses in General Dynamics' program soon came to light. On June 11, 1972, *Seattle Times* reporter Clark Mollenhoff reported that General Dynamics was in legal trouble concerning the TFX contract. The company and four of its present and former executives were indicted by a grand jury "on charges of fraud involving the cost of defective parts for the controversial F-111 fighter-bomber."

These discoveries were not new. "The hearing record established by Senator John McClellan's Permanent Investigating Subcommittee laid out much of the evidence of misleading reports, inaccurate testimony under oath and conflicts of interest as early as 1963 and 1964, documenting events that involved the credibility of our highest officials," Mollenhoff reported.

The conflict of interest appeared to be that the Deputy Secretary of Defense, Roswell Gilpatrick, and the Secretary of the Navy had close ties to General Dynamics and to a Fort Worth bank that financed the company.

Richard Geer finished his account of the TFX saga with these comments:

> Oddly enough, the McNamara decision split the F-111 production line between the F-111A at Forth Worth and the F-111B at Bethpage, much to the anguish of Albert W. Blackburn, the former F-111 project officer in the Office of the Director, Defense Research and Engineering. Earlier McNamara had vetoed separate lines for the F-4B and F-4C, on the grounds of commonality. . . . As of February 1968, Secretary McNamara was by no means sure the F-111B [for the Navy] would last much past his departure from the Defense Department, and March 28, the Senate Armed Services Committee voted 11 to 2 to withhold funds for the F-111B development.

The Supersonic Transport (SST) project was also a heart-breaker. The concept of a supersonic plane dates back to at least 1953, when the idea was proposed by the Air Force in what was called the "Weapon System 110A" competition. This would be for a huge new bomber capable of supersonic flight. By November of that year the competition had been whittled down to Boeing versus North American. The Boeing engineers believed they might win because they had put a lot of effort into solving the crucial heat and structural problems involved in supersonic flying. Ed was under intense pressure because Allen had said Boeing must win this one.

In March 1956 the Air Force announced that neither Boeing nor North American had turned in a suitable proposal and the competition would be continued in order to seek improvements in design.

George Schairer, assistant chief engineer at that time, told his engineers to scrub the plan and start anew, and from the many (some almost bizarre) designs proposed, they did come up with a design quite similar to one that had been proposed two years before, a stainless steel plane that had an intercontinental range flying at three times the speed of sound. Boeing had begun to build a $30 million Developmental Center in 1955, in anticipation of winning this contract. Boeing planners were so confident they decided to shift the production of B-52s almost entirely to Wichita to leave the Seattle plant available for the supersonic project.

An Air Force representative came in 1955 to check on progress. He hinted that the two competing companies were running neck-and-neck in the race, both having achieved "major break-throughs." Ed was getting a bit nervous; the waiting seemed so long. Then, just two days before Christmas the final decision was announced: North American was given the contract to build the ill-fated B-70. (Only two were ever built, one of which crashed. The other is now on display in the Air Force Museum at Wright-Patterson Air Force Base in Dayton.)

Boeing's Transport Division then turned its attention to a supersonic transport. Lloyd Goodmanson, project aerodynamicist on the TFX, was named to head up the project, and work intensified in the summer of 1958. Work on the TFX had put Boeing far ahead in the development of a unique honeycomb structure to strengthen a lightweight stainless steel wing. Boeing had even received a sub-contract from North American to build the wings of its B-70 bomber using this process.

But the Boeing design for the supersonic transport still had a major flaw. According to wind tunnel results and paper figures, the

Mockup of the SST, demonstrating the variable sweep wing (*Boeing P40448*)

plane would fly at supersonic speeds, but embarrassingly enough, it could neither take off nor land at safe subsonic speeds. In March there was a dramatic breakthrough. The famous aerodynamicist John Stack called Boeing about something at NASA's Langley Labs they'd like to show someone. Stack's innovation was a hinge that made the variable sweep achievable, with a severely swept-back wing in flight and a normally positioned wing for takeoff and landing. Boeing engineers now worked feverishly inventing all sorts of "hinges" to get the one just right to sweep back those wings and to reposition them for takeoffs and landings. The more they tested, the more enthusiastic they became.

The government's cancellation of the North American B-70 contract also ended Boeing's contract to produce B-70 wings, and the pivot-jointed swept-back wing on the new Boeing design for the SST made the honeycomb process unnecessary. The Boeing engineers went back to the usual construction for airplane wings, this time using titanium for lightness and strength. Titanium also could withstand the extreme heat that supersonic flight entails.

SST titanium wing hinge (*Boeing P35356*)

In the summer of 1963, Boeing learned that the European Con-corde supersonic commercial transport was being put together with subsidies from the governments of Great Britain and France. Ed made several trips to Sud Aviation in Toulouse to learn about the project. His research was aided by the fact that in the years since his first trip to Europe in 1949 he had resumed the study of French—which he had taken in high school—and had also taken up German, Spanish, and Italian. "My lack of communication abili-ty on the [first] trip bothered me greatly," he recalled. "Only one thing bothered me more, and that was the discovery that the Unit-ed States was being represented . . . by hundreds and thousands of people, military and civil, who knew little if any more than I did of any language other than English."

By the time he visited Sud Aviation he was able to discuss the Concorde in fluent French, an achievement which improved his understanding of the project and gave him great satisfaction.

President Kennedy announced that he would like to see a joint
effort by the American government and industry to build a supersonic transport to compete with the Concorde. On August 13, 1963,
the FAA invited American aviation companies to submit proposals
for a supersonic transport "superior to the European plane," aim-
ing at three times rather than twice the speed of sound, and using
titanium instead of aluminum. Ed was pleased with this approach.
Douglas bowed out of the competition, but Lockheed, North American, and Boeing eagerly entered.

A conference was called back at Langley Labs so that the three
competitors could discuss the virtues of the delta wing and the
variable-sweep wing along with two other possibilities. Boeing assigned a group to each design to study and test. The variable-
sweep wing turned out to produce a plane 50,000 pounds lighter,
and Ed chose it. North American and Lockheed both decided to en-
ter a delta-wing configuration in the competition.

In the midst of the work on the SST, Ed received the last of his
weekly letters from his father. Edward Lansing Wells was in frail
health at age eighty-eight. He had recently moved to the home of
his daughter Alice in Pendleton, Oregon. There he could be under
the care of her husband, Dr. Jack Grondahl, who was a general
practitioner. On December 31, 1963, Wells wrote to Ed:

> Not till late in the afternoon did I remember that this is the day to write to
> you.
>   Things have not been going so well with me as could be wished. Jack
> is trying all sorts of things to enable me to eat and drink to keep up my
> strength, and has, I think had some success. But I am still not getting
> down enough food and drink to keep up my strength. He may put me on
> Metrical or put me in the hospital for intravenous feeding.
>   It worries other folks a lot more than it worries me.
>   I didn't feel able to go to church Sunday, but heard the service over the
> radio. The "sermon" was by three college students, one of them was
> Molly [his granddaughter]. Instead of complaining about the conditions
> in the colleges, she told what students can do to improve conditions. . . .
>   Christmas was a great day for me. Forty-six years ago today I left Boise
> for Portland.

Shortly thereafter Wells was diagnosed with stomach cancer. He
underwent surgery but died in the recovery room on January 10.

Laura Wells had died in 1962 at the age of ninety-three. There
would be no more of those weekly letters and those special ones on
birthdays and anniversaries that had been faithfully written by our
father to his children from the day they left home. But Ed had kept a

file of the special ones, and one of the most treasured had come dated May 8, 1945, celebrating the victory of the Allies in Europe. After starting out with, "V-E Day has arrived and it is gratifying to know that you have played a very important part in hastening it," the letter goes on to recall that on that day our father had come across a speech he had made at a father-son banquet when Ed was about ten or eleven years old (when Ed had been making model airplanes, crude steam engines out of discarded tin cans, and the pirate ship). The parts of the speech as quoted in the letter were revealing of the relationship between father and son:

> Did you ever see a wild bird in a cage, beating its wings and breaking its feathers against the cruel bars that held it down? That bird was made to fly and to sing and to do a lot of things it cannot do in its cage.
> Did you ever stop to think that the soul of a man is like that? There were a thousand things that your soul wants to do that it cannot do.
> Your soul says "build," but your hand is unskilled and the plans you try to draw are condemned even by your own imperfect standard. But when you see your boy, with hand that is steady and eye that is true, and a mind that sees the end of a structure before it is yet begun, you know that some day the world will look on the monument which his skill has erected to your soul's desire.

Of all the many honors and awards Ed was to receive during his lifetime, none brought stronger emotion than this expression of our father's love, confidence, and pride.

On January 21, 1964, eleven days after Ed's father's death, Maynard Pennell presented Boeing's case for the SST to the FAA. He argued that with Boeing's variable-sweep, the SST could fly without the characteristic sonic noise over cities and could obtain a speed of 800 mph at 45,000 feet, 1,450 mph at 50,000 feet, and 1,800 mph at 60,000 feet. Pennell also claimed that the plane could be operated at approximately the same cost as jet transports then flying.

After all competitors had made their presentations, the FAA began its deliberations. The agency then asked for a Phase II presentation to be submitted in 1965. Boeing reshaped the body of the plane, increasing passenger capacity, and further refined its aerodynamics. Pennell now said that seat-mile cost would be lower than on subsonic planes on all but the shortest routes. The aircraft industry hoped the FAA would authorize construction of prototypes before the European Concorde got too far ahead.

Washington, D.C., began buzzing with rumors and questions. Would a supersonic transport bring disaster to the jet plane travel industry? Would it poison the environment? The FAA again stalled, announcing that the project would have to go into its next phase before the agency would give permission for prototype production. In July 1965, another delay of eighteen months was proposed, with a continuation of design consideration and testing before a prototype was built. The companies involved would bear one-fourth of the cost, subject to reimbursement if the program was abandoned. And in the end it was abandoned: On March 24, 1971, Congress responded to public pressure and refused to appropriate further funding. "Probably the right decision for all the wrong reasons," Ed told the Society of Automotive Engineers in 1980. "I do not doubt that it would have been a significantly better SST than its predecessors, but only in the sense that its huge operating losses would have been less than those of its competitors." The SST would have used huge amounts of fuel, and the OPEC oil embargo in 1973 and subsequent rise in gas prices would have made Pennell's optimistic seat-per-mile estimates obsolete. The late 1980s saw an interest in developing SSTs for both military and commercial use, but the program has yet to be actively revived.

For Ed the successes far outweighed disappointments like the SST. Perhaps one of the secrets of his success lay in his selfless commitment to accomplishment. George Schairer said that "it never occurred to Ed Wells to think with egotism. It never occurred to him to emphasize the personal in, 'Can I do it?' He always challenged himself with, 'Can it be done?'" No matter how tough the problem, he had an infectious kind of optimism that "it can be done."

With all the peaks of success and the valleys of discouragement through which the Boeing Company went while Ed was working there, he maintained a fierce loyalty toward the company, even though he was offered very flattering inducements to transfer his talent elsewhere. One of the most memorable and flamboyant offers came from Howard Hughes. Hughes often called Ed, night or day, for the answer to some question on flying or on building planes. In 1939 Hughes purchased a Boeing Stratoliner "for research purposes," after he had visited the Seattle Boeing plant and had been given a demonstration flight with Eddie Allen at the controls. Actually that plane became a very expensive Hughes "toy"— in two years it had twenty hours of flight time. (Hughes did buy five for TWA.)

Sometime about 1957 or 1958 Hughes asked Ed to come to Los Angeles for a talk. Ed was somewhat reluctant because Hughes usually had some movie star or starlet on his arm, and Ed was out of his element with Hollywood chatter. On this particular occasion Ed was sharing a room at a hotel with his associate, George Schairer, while they were in Los Angeles on Boeing business. Schairer loves to tell the story. He said he became quite worried when 3 a.m. came and Wells had not yet returned to the room. When he did arrive he said, "I think we finally had run out of nightclubs to attend and with the starlets we had long since run out of reasonable conversation topics to discuss, so I finally made my 'adieux'—but when I got down to my rented car I found I did not have the keys. I had to sneak back to the nightclub and grope under the table as unobtrusively as I could to find the keys on the floor."

On the next date Hughes came without the starlets, and during the evening he offered a salary of $500,000 per year if Ed would move to southern California to head up Hughes Aircraft. The contract offered was for an initial period of five years. At this time Ed was a house guest in my home in Los Angeles. When he arrived that night, completely exhausted from the interview, he said that "the longer Hughes talked or the more I was persuaded that I never could work for the man. For some reason he didn't seem to be able to take 'no' for an answer."

To the outsider, the Boeing Company seems always to be reorganizing, announcing new departments or divisions and renaming them, and switching their executives from one position to another. From 1961 through 1970, Ed was vice president/general manager in Military Aircraft Systems. Then this was merged with Transport to become the Airplane Division, and he became vice president of the Airplane Division, then vice president/product development, and next, senior vice president/technical.

After Ed retired from Boeing as senior vice president in 1971, he stayed on as a consultant "on call." In 1980, he was the featured speaker at a banquet for the Society of Automotive Engineers' Aerospace Congress and Exposition. After a summary of aviation history as he had lived it, he looked toward the future. Always a realist, he discussed what could be accomplished under conditions of deregulation, rising energy costs, and slow economic growth:

> The current recession has slowed economic growth and in turn has had an adverse effect on air transport profitability. So-called "deregulation" has had what sometimes seems to be a compounding adverse economic effect, as competitors scramble vigorously for a share of the more slowly growing market. Hopefully, this situation will stabilize. . . .

I believe that a reasonable projection into the future would indicate that an SST can survive economically only:

1. If energy costs do not continue to rise dramatically.

2. If there is an adequate market in intercontinental travel at a significant premium in fare.

3. If there are significant advances in commercially applicable technology, in particular in structures, aerodynamics and propulsion.

4. If there are enough financially solvent airlines who believe in the future of the SST and will purchase it in quantities sufficient to make a program economically viable without direct subsidy.

I think that you will agree that these are rather severe qualifications, and that if they are correct, a lot of time may elapse before we see another SST ready for commercial service.

Next, what might be expected in subsonic transport development? Here again, economics is the name of the game in designing our vehicles and operating systems, the difference being that the subsonic transport has a fighting chance of making the grade.

By 1985, efficient fan [fanjet]-powered airplanes benefiting from up-to-date airframe, systems and propulsion technology should be available for all usable ranges and for all sizes from about 150 passengers up [high-density seating].

I'm not so optimistic as to believe, however, that the aircraft and airline industries will have won all their economic battles at that point. Economics as the name of the game is going to be with us for a long time to come, and it will present a tremendous challenge, out of which will come winners and some losers and possibly some mergers.

The results may well be judged by factors such as:

1. The ability to use energy more efficiently as energy costs escalate.

2. The ability to control labor intensive costs.

3. The ability to judge whether so-called "frills" are non-productive or productive.

4. The ability to make air cargo contribute significantly to revenue.

5. The ability to avoid costly, undisciplined competition.

6. The ability to achieve effective equipment utilization.

7. The ability to schedule to achieve profitable load factors.

8. The ability to attract traffic in spite of increasing transportation costs.

9. The ability to maintain reliability of equipment and scheduling.

10. The ability to control the cost of equipment in relation to its productivity and its useful operating life.

11. The ability to demonstrate a dedication to safety in all aspects of design, manufacture and operation.

12. The ability to incorporate proven new technology contributing to economic operation with safety, reliability and convenience.

To deal with these and other factors successfully will require the best possible performance by designers, manufacturers, operators and regulating agencies.

Toward that end, designers and manufacturers should concentrate on improving the reliability and economics of all models; operators should concentrate on convenient service with reliability and economy; and regulating agencies should apply their controls with intelligence and fairness.

With sufficient attention and a modest amount of good luck, the current and new airplanes coming into service through 1985 can survive economically, and even more important, they can provide a stable economic base for the continuing development and growth of commercial air transport.

Assuming a stable base, it might be reasonable to go beyond mere speculation on what is to come beyond 1985. Before us is an impressive shopping list of possible improvements. These include:

1. More efficient engines.
2. Quieter propulsion systems.
3. Alternative fuels.
4. Improved structural alloys.
5. Advanced composites.
6. Advanced avionics, instrumentation, control systems.
7. Improved aerodynamics.
8. Computer-aided design and manufacturing.
9. Improved traffic control—ground and air.
10. Wise use of regulatory authority.

If we can carry out the necessary research and development, if we can incorporate the best results intelligently into our design, if we can operate our equipment to maximize its productivity and if we can achieve a proper balance between over-regulation and under-regulation, I, for one, see a bright future for the aircraft and air transport industries. May we have the hindsight, the foresight and the wisdom to put it all together right for another seventy-five years!

10

Final Years

In his beautiful book, *Boeing B-52,* Walter Boyne has included thumbnail sketches of the men who were involved in the design and production of that bomber. The profile of Ed Wells notes that "despite his incredible career and many awards, he remains a courteous, soft-spoken man who continually deprecates his own contributions, while signaling out others for their work. He is extremely precise in his choice of words and has a tremendously broad overview of not only aviation and space, but also economics and politics. Boeing was fortunate to have him, and in many ways he typifies the company—a doer rather than a talker."

Ed's life outside work followed the same pattern. His open-mindedness, wide interests, and focused attention all enriched his personal activities as well as his work. And underlying his many talents was a firm moral foundation. He was quietly and deeply religious.

Our father had been particularly influential in Ed's religious attitudes. The influence was mutual, for Father always said, "My children liberalized me." As the Methodist Church broadened its viewpoint, the elder Wells became more liberal and Ed Wells was more comfortable in it. Dorothy Wells's background was also Methodist, an ancestor of hers being a minister in the Norwegian Methodist Church. So Dorothy and Ed Wells started their married life as members of the Methodist Church in Seattle.

While living in the Mount Baker neighborhood, they transferred their membership to the Mount Baker Presbyterian Church so that their children could attend church with their neighborhood friends. Ed even became moderator, although he never was entirely comfortable with Calvinist theology. Nor was he ever at ease with the concept of the communion service. (He just didn't attend on the Sundays when a Eucharist was on the schedule.)

When the Wells family moved to Bellevue, they joined the First Congregational Church there. One of the biggest undertakings Ed supervised in this church was the moving of the entire building to change the orientation of the sanctuary. He also took on the responsibility of helping a minister with a personal problem. The minister had become an alcoholic and had lost his pastorate and his wife. Wells became a caring friend, getting him into a rehabilitation program, finding him a job at Boeing, and "holding his hand." The man later became a professional counselor on drug abuse and alcoholism, rejoined his church and, for the rest of his life, counseled young people very successfully, always saying, "To Ed Wells I owe my life and the resurrection of my soul."

Ed's religion was always a personal matter that did not require outward display. Once after attending a memorial service in a Friends Meeting, where one sits in silence until the Spirit moves someone to speak, he confided to Dorothy that "I believe I could be very happy in that kind of religion."

In a speech on "Self-Critical Questions," part of a symposium on Space and Christianity held during the Century 21 Exposition in Seattle in 1961, Ed addressed some of the conflicts between technology and religious belief. The influence of his father can be recognized in both the content and the phrasing of these excerpts:

Dr. Pollard [the previous speaker] has made each one of us feel, as perhaps we had not before, an emotion of gratitude for the privilege of living in this age of scientific and material achievement. But he has at the same time reminded us forcefully that in our headlong progress in this one direction, we risk losing our way entirely. Truly we do live in a world of magnificent material and physical advancement. Just as truly, however, we do sometimes lack an awareness of what Dr. Pollard has termed the supernatural—that awareness so essential to a balanced existence, particularly in such a rapidly moving world.

For some, the scientific or material achievement serves to quicken the pace toward the next assault on the material unknown, but for many, the purely material achievement will inevitably bring into focus our inability to be self-sufficient—our need for spiritual as well as material growth....

True, many of the daily events of our time could bring despair to the most optimistic mind. At the same time, however, we can be encouraged by signs on the positive side of the ledger. These signs give me hope that the renaissance can and may well be under way in Century 20, if we who otherwise might stand and wait for Century 21 and its great promise would instead extend ourselves to be effective in Century 20. The very magnitude of the progress toward scientific understanding in Century 20, the very wonders of the natural world which unfold before our eyes in scientific exhibits and elsewhere, can only eventually force increasing attention on those areas in which we are failing to make comparable advances.

Why, we may well ask, with such material progress must a spiritual awakening be further delayed? Why not, at least, a glimpse of a new horizon in Century 20, in our generation rather than the next? . . .

What are the obstacles which we might effectively help to remove? Let me pose a few self-critical questions to illustrate:

Have we as professing Christians ever made a God of material, while professing to "have no other Gods before Thee"?

Have scientists, in pursuit of either scientific understanding or individual achievement, ever overemphasized the scientific, the natural, the human achievement elements of our world to the exclusion of the extra-scientific and supernatural? . . .

Have men of religion, with their deep understanding of things spiritual and theological, set up a God apart, a God little understood and often not accepted by others?

Do we ever insist on defining the supernatural exclusively in terms of our own limited experience, demanding literal acceptance by others? Is this not an approach fully as dangerous as a dogmatic approach in science?

As professing Christians, confronted by a decision of moral or ethical nature, have we ever rationalized or shrugged our shoulders at compromise in principle by others?

Have we ever forgotten Christ's counsel—"As you did it to one of the least of these my brethren, you did it to me?"

Have we ever been proud when humility would have been more appropriate? Have we ever been belligerent when we should have been compassionate?

Unhappily, we must answer too often in the affirmative. It is my conviction that the ultimate timing of the renaissance will largely be determined by our willingness to face the implications of these and other self-critical questions. . . .

The supernatural and its spiritual reality do exist, and they will continue to exist without end—our actions and our thoughts can in no way destroy their existence. But just as surely human action, thought and deed are required if a spiritual rebirth is to take place. God in his infinite wisdom has left it to us to find the human means with which to make a heaven on earth. The supernatural may continue to exist apart, without substantially affecting the human family, or it may burst into our consciousness, enrich our lives, change the course of history. . . .

As far as politics were concerned, Ed proclaimed himself in another speech as "independent, sometimes for lack of decision, sometimes for ignorance, sometimes for utter frustration, sometimes by deliberate and reasoning choice.... I have made contributions to candidates of both parties on the basis of known capabilities of individual candidates. I have yet to make a contribution willingly or purposefully to either party as a party. I have never voted a straight ticket for either party, nor do I expect to in my lifetime."

Ed did have strong opinions—mostly liberal—but his friends would always say, "He never said a negative word about anybody," and unless asked point-blank, he would never suggest concerning behavior, religion, or politics what another human being should think or do.

Although Ed devoted himself wholeheartedly to his work and other commitments, he never lost sight of the rest of life's pleasures, and his retirement gave him time to pursue his many other interests. The model trains that had delighted his children and their neighbors on Cascadia Avenue evidently were left behind when the family moved to Bellevue, but many other projects took their place.

The French language study that he began in order to represent Boeing better overseas was followed by lessons in Italian, German, Portuguese, and Spanish. He found German to be the most difficult language, but even in German he did well. In fact, Dr. Alfred Steiglitz, who was in charge of the Seattle Berlitz School and would later be in charge of texts for national Berlitz programs, decided Ed would be an ideal first subject to try out the new concept of Berlitz's "total immersion" method of learning a language. This method uses six or seven teachers who speak conversationally in the language in a 72-hour session in the presence of the student. The premise is that, being "monkeys" to a certain extent, persons in frustration have to "ape" the language, trying to express themselves as they begin to understand what is being said. It worked with Ed and German, and Berlitz began to offer the program internationally with all languages.

"In the beginning," Ed recalled, "my enthusiasm and resolve were not matched certainly by my fluency, particularly in German and Italian, but the reward for effort was there. The 1958 trip was ever so much more rewarding and productive than that of 1949, and by 1960, when we had an extensive trip through much of the same area... I was really beginning to receive the dividends in better communication and understanding."

Ed's Berlitz study yielded an added dividend, because he and Dorothy met as their teacher a young giant of a Frenchman who would become a cherished friend. Jean-Claude Peter was studying business administration on a Fulbright scholarship at the University of Washington and supplementing his stipend by working as a waiter and teaching at Berlitz. Ed, in the end, became extremely fluent, and he and his young teacher liked to exchange ribald jokes and puns in French. The Wellses kept in close touch with Jean-Claude and his family over the years. Jean-Claude was always annoyed when he heard Ed Wells spoken of as a shy man, because the Wells he knew was so warm, fun-loving, and outgoing.

As time became available, the Wellses began to travel more for pleasure. A business trip to South America in 1964 led to several pleasure trips to Mexico, visits that Ed recorded both in photography and landscape painting.

Our mother had been an amateur photographer when we lived in Boise, spreading her glass negatives on cardboard boxes in the yard to expose in the sunlight and worrying that we children would overturn them during a game of tag. Among the family memorabilia are a few of these glass plates and some fading photos kept as memories of "when father and mother were young."

Ed was too small at the time to remember her hobby in any vivid detail, but in his own forties photography became a favored pursuit. Coupled with painting and travel, these intertwined interests became what he called a "three-way hobby": travel to learn of the world; photography to remember what has been seen; and sketches or paintings to express the emotion which the travel aroused. He provided himself with excellent camera equipment, including a miniature camera about the size of two matchboxes, which despite its size produced high-resolution slides which projected well.

Very early in life Ed had begun to draw pictures, filling cheap pencil tablets in quantities. Among the things found in those four boxes of his "life history" was a pencil sketch (at age three) of the "Jello Belt Line" trolley which circled Boise at the time. And there was (drawn at five) a solemn portrait of his father with goatee, moustache, and hat, while in the background is pictured the children's playhouse and the chopping stump upon which Ed's father split the wood to fuel the kitchen range and the wood burning stoves.

His first painting was done in oil—a rather crude one of the Grand Canyon of the Yellowstone. It was made after a family visit to Yellowstone National Park. At the same time he did a remarkable ink drawing of Old Faithful. During high school and college days, Wells did some other fine drawings of architectural subjects, auto-

Landscape drawn by Ed during high school days after a family vacation trip

mobiles of his own design, and at least one original design of a plane. He was always self-taught, never having had a lesson (except mechanical drawing) in drawing, painting, or carving, and he reveled in experimenting with all kinds of art media.

After a long hiatus, he resumed painting upon his retirement. "I found that my oil painting kit was in pretty bad shape, and that my watercolors were nowhere to be found, so I was in no position to pick up immediately where I had left off some fifteen years before," he said. "Instead of rushing out and buying new oils, brushes, knives, canvas and thinner, I undertook a study of current painting media for both opaque and transparent colors and decided that for opaque colors I much preferred the acrylic medium to the oils I had previously used. In the spring of 1972 I began to paint regularly in opaque acrylics, using some of my travel photographs as subject matter. Toward the end of 1972, I expanded my study and experimentation into the field of transparent watercolors, and as a result decided to embark experimentally at last into watercolor painting, using transparent acrylic watercolors as the medium in preference to 'traditional' watercolors."

On their fortieth wedding anniversary Ed and Dorothy decided to visit places in Europe they had not seen before. They began with looking for places where Dorothy's ancestors had lived in Norway and Sweden. This trip finally ended in the south of France with an

Ed's oil painting of Pont-de-Montvert, France

inspection of that little-visited part of France, the Cevennes, with which Ed became charmed, and some time spent in the marshy Camargue area at the delta of the Rhone. Ed's photographs and paintings preserved his impressions of these new sights.

On his Boeing assignments, Ed had always been put up in such swank Paris hotels as the Plaza-Athenée and the George V. Now that they were on their own and Ed had become fluent in French, they decided to travel as the ordinary French do. Touring the country, as they would see an attractive country hotel or inn, they would present themselves at the desk and be taken in with warmth and welcome. And it worked, much to their delight if not surprise.

Ed and Dorothy also took two trips, on their own, to Australia, and were fascinated with what they saw. On another trip through the United States, they looked in on all the spots their ancestors were known to have lived in Montana, North and South Dakota, Wisconsin, Iowa, Kentucky, and Virginia.

Ed had always toyed with the idea of someday being able to return to Stanford to teach a little, and in 1969–70 his dream was realized. He was invited to Stanford for that school year to conduct a graduate seminar in engineering topics. During that year he also found both time and inspiration to paint. "Our Palo Alto apartment complex was set among huge oak and eucalyptus trees," he said. "On a walk one day, the play of light through the trees caught my attention. One of our grandsons, then ten years old, was visiting, and one day we started out for a walk toward town along the dusty tree-lined road paralleling the creek. As the boy started out ahead, eager to get there first, I snapped a picture and decided that since it had been twenty years since I had painted a human subject, here was one I could try to put on canvas."

After Ed's death, Boeing endowed the Edward C. Wells Chair in Aeronautics and Astronautics at Stanford. The endowment, which will total $1.6 million, was presented on January 26, 1990, at a dinner hosted by Boeing executives in Seattle and attended by members of Ed's family and Stanford professors.

One of the bonuses he realized from his interests in art and travel was the rapport they brought him with his children. Laurie Jo had graduated in fine arts from Stanford and had studied art one summer at the University of Guadalajara; Edward Elliott had graduated from the University of Washington with a major in geography; and the grandsons were interested in travel, having done a great deal of it themselves.

In 1985, Laurie Jo wrote a tribute to her father's talents:

Edward Curtis Wells liked to draw, design and build things, especially mechanical things, from the time he was a small boy. Now, at age seventy-five, he has been painting with acrylics steadily for a number of years, but his canvases, most often 16" by 20", are of landscapes rather than airplane designs such as those on which his fame in aviation industry is based. . . .

The natural surroundings of the homes of his children in Colorado and in rural Northern California have been the focus of many of his paintings. On foreign travels he has taken photographs of forests in Scotland, Monet's garden at Giverny in France, the Australian desert, the sea and fjords of Scandinavia and the softly colored adobe buildings on village streets in Mexico.

Ed Wells, inventor and scientist that he is, experiments with the mixing and juxtaposition of colors. He sometimes paints the same scene more than once, slightly altering the design. He uses retarding medium and attains with acrylics an unusually glowing, soft quality more often associated with oils. In some paintings he obtains a brightness and light in his blue or lightly clouded skies by starting out with an undercoat of yellow ocher mixed with white and a gel medium.

Not surprisingly, the boats, bridges, barns and other buildings which sometimes appear in his paintings, he has lovingly rendered with architectural precision; but the great variety of subtle color found in meadows and fields, or the light-dappled and umber-shadowed foliage of trees are more often his subjects. His rural landscapes in particular gently project a quiet solitude and sometimes a faint aura of mystery.

Ed Wells, self-taught as a painter, has never devoted any one period of his life to painting nor has he attempted to market his work, but his many canvases (over 100) completed in "spare time" before and after his retirement, attest that art as well as science and the airplane industry might well have been a successful career. Over the years his family and friends have been afforded much pleasure because he chose painting as one important way to express his enormous creativity.

Among the additional interests in the last years of Ed's life were astronomy and astro-photography. He and Dorothy were supporters of the Friends of the Planetarium, a group formed through the efforts of a close friend to provide the expensive equipment for the planetarium building at Bellevue Community College. In a speech to the Friends, he described the human perspective provided by a study of the sky:

Some feeling for the small part of the universe occupied by our Earth and its sun can be obtained when we realize that the stars next nearest to us are 270,000 times more distant than the sun, or 40 trillion kilometers....

These vast distances and deep mysteries of the universe have always fascinated me, but my interest remained dormant until a little over two years ago, when one of my grandsons, then eleven years old, began to ask questions and to look for reading material on the subject of astronomy. To help his interest, I gave him a basic 60mm aperture refractor telescope on an equatorial mount....On each visit I watched the night sky with him and, before long, I found myself "hooked" on a new hobby.

The next step was a big one—not one but two 20-cm aperture reflector telescopes, one for the grandson on his 13th birthday and one for me to keep me busy in Bellevue between visits to Northern California. These telescopes were quite well equipped to begin with, but I now know that buying a telescope is like buying a boat—it's the accessories that will kill you if you are not disciplined.

In 1979 Ed's name came up, apparently for the third time, as a candidate for the coveted Daniel Guggenheim Medal award. When, in 1980, he was notified that he had been chosen for that year's award, he confided to me: "It was the one which would mean the most to me, and I had given up hope I would ever get it." His citation reads, "For his outstanding contributions to the management concepts for the development of large aerospace systems, and for his significant personal accomplishments in the design and production of a long line of the world's most famous commercial and military aircraft."

He was the fifth Boeing executive to receive the award, following William Boeing in 1934, Eddie Allen in 1943, George Schairer in 1967, and William Allen in 1973. Other famous recipients include Donald Douglas, Glenn L. Martin, Juan Trippe, Jimmy Doolittle, Sir Frank Whittle, and Charles Lindbergh.

That same year, Ed severed his relationship as a consultant with Boeing. He found that the consultant status qualified him as "self-employed" under Washington state tax law, and he confessed there was "just too much red tape involved to make it worthwhile."

In 1983, the Museum of Flight at Boeing Field, Seattle, presented its second Pathfinder Award to six pioneers of flight. Ed was the only living honoree. The award mentioned "41 years with Boeing, developing the B-17, B-29, B-47 and B-52, as well as the 707 prototype." In 1985 Ed received the Tony Jannus Award "for outstanding contributions to commercial aviation."

"Ed is one of those movers and innovators whose original thinking and organizational abilities and drive have spurred the pace of change in the world today," said presenter Knut Hammerskjold. "And all of us involved in aviation owe a tremendous debt of gratitude."

When Ed and Dorothy were looking forward to retirement and longer periods away from home, they decided to sell their waterfront home and to look for a condominium with a security system at the entrance gate. They found one at a lovely place called "Sans Souci." It didn't turn out to be exactly "Without Care," for Ed, being the successful manager of affairs he had always been, was the obvious choice to head every committee the "condo" tenants needed: for repairs, for settling rental misunderstandings, etc. He assumed the chores cheerfully, because both Ed and Dorothy liked these congenial neighbors and they lived comfortably in this location for a number of happy years. But astronomy became so important to Ed that he needed a place with an unobstructed view of the sky and a place where he could have a shop adequate to house his lathe (for years in "moth balls"), drill press, and his other tools. He wanted to make accessories for his telescopes—accessories of his own design and specifications.

They found a house on the high west side of Somerset Hill above

Bellevue, with a clear view of the sky and beautiful panoramic view of the city of Seattle, Lake Washington, and the Olympic Mountains as a backdrop.

They bought the house in 1983, had some remodeling done, and in the backyard Ed erected a concrete permanent mounting for his now very sophisticated telescope. This mounting made possible all the experimentation in astro-photography Ed could wish for, and he spent many hours at night perfecting his skills. "One of the best nights in the entire year was one of those clear nights in early February with the temperature hovering around −10° Celsius," he said. "This was a good test of my amateur will to persist and to see and photograph when half-frozen."

After considerable research, Ed also bought a home computer plus accessories and software. He then bought a stack of instruction books and began, as usual, to teach himself all about how to use it. After he got well into his learning, he found he could scarcely pull himself away from the machine or the printout. He grinned, "It's addictive!"

If Ed Wells was private about religion and uncommitted in politics, he was neither when it came to automobiles. When he was in high school he had been entranced with the Dodge touring car (the kind with button-on side curtains) that was the family's first car purchase. He had daydreamed as he drew his own imaginary cars. Among the papers found after his death are beautiful sketches of these cars done during high school years. In his first year of permanent employment at Boeing, he had bought that little secondhand coupe, which was followed by Studebakers, Volkswagens, Renaults, and other makes, but in late years there was a devotion to Mercedes. Ed and his son, as Dorothy reported, "bought all the car magazines as soon as they came off the presses."

In the summer of 1985, Wells looked at a Toyota Camry and fell deeply in love. He bought one and proudly showed it to anyone who would listen. "This one has everything! Just look at that! And this!" He had decided that the engineering in even the smallest detail was near perfection. The next spring, Dorothy and Ed decided to give it a trial shakedown with a trip to southern California for a visit to relatives and to two of Ed's graduate students, who had become close friends during his teaching stint at Stanford.

He had been having some vague abdominal discomfort, so the trip was postponed until a complete physical examination could be made. After barium x-ray tests were performed, the family physician said, "You're fine as far as I can see. Call me if you think you're dying."

On the trip the Camry met all of Ed's expectations, but by the time he and Dorothy reached the home of our sister Peggy in Sun City, California, he found he was in discomfort after each meal. The two continued on to Palm Springs, and the next morning Ed awoke with a definite abdominal edema. They hurried over to consult with doctors at the Eisenhower Medical Center.

After a lengthy and exhausting CAT scan test, the doctors gave Ed the bad news: pancreatic cancer as a strong possibility. A biopsy sample was obtained and the diagnosis confirmed. The doctors told Ed and Dorothy that it would probably be terminal, and suggested that they might prefer to return to Seattle for any further treatment. They decided to fly back to Seattle for treatment at the Arnold Tumor Clinic and Swedish Hospital, of excellent reputation in oncology care.

Wells was checked in at Swedish Hospital, where the excess fluid accumulation was drained, making him temporarily more comfortable. Further tests held out a bit of hope: tissue samples showed that Wells had a rare type of pancreatic cancer, which in 50 percent of cases responds well to chemotherapy. The doctors scheduled two treatments four weeks apart, after which they would evaluate the results of treatment. In addition, an operation was performed to implant a very ingenious "shunt pump" called the Laveen Shunt, which carries excess fluid from the abdominal cavity back into the blood stream where nourishment (especially protein) that would otherwise be lost could be utilized. This implant brought enormous relief and Ed was able to return home.

Although the chemotherapy treatment did not cause the anticipated nausea, it did cause acute loss of appetite and weakness. At times Ed was returned to the hospital for intravenous feeding.

Toward the end of April, two and a half months after the initial diagnosis, the physicians determined that the tumor was not responding to treatment. Ed elected to discontinue the chemotherapy. His appetite improved, but the weakness and fatigue continued to increase. A program of home hospice care was set up by the hospital, and Ed began to set his affairs in order.

Dorothy and Ed talked over where she would live when he was gone, and he chose the real estate agent who would handle the sale of the house for her. He arranged for an automatic sprinkler system to be installed to water the shrubs and lawn, and he hired professional gardeners to care for the yard. He called in his very good friend, Dale Turner, a retired Congregational minister, who was a fellow member of a men's dinner group in Seattle and was now a regular columnist for the *Seattle Times*. Turner had said before, "I always saw to it that I arrived early for the dinner meeting so I could sit next to Ed Wells, for he always had such interesting things to say. I loved him like my own brother."

When he left the hospital for the last time at the end of April, the doctors gave a prognosis of from one to four months to live. The flowers and letters and telephone calls and cards poured in. One was a tribute from one of Ed's nephews, which read, "As a boy and even as I grew older, I was looking for a hero to emulate, then suddenly I realized I had one in you, Ed." The hospice nurses were angels of skilled caring and support and became close friends.

Ed Wells never showed himself so loving and so strong as during these months of discomfort, debilitating fatigue, and sadness. In the last few days, strength was ebbing and morphine was administered to ease the pain, but the smile still remained strong. As was mentioned earlier, the children of Edward Lansing and Laura Long Wells had early learned to weep with joy at good fortune but to be dry-eyed and strong when disaster threatened to strike them down.

It seemed as if Ed Wells, the seventy-five-year-old man, was reaching back in memory to the little lad who had held so tightly to his father's hand so long ago on those Sunday afternoon hikes in the Boise foothills, when the father was patiently teaching the little boy to memorize, in preparation for these last days, William Cullen Bryant's "Thanatopsis":

> 'So live, that when thy summons comes to join
> The innumerable caravan which moves
> To that mysterious realm, where each shall take
> His place in the silent hall of death,
> Thou go not, like the quarry slave at night,
> Scourged to his dungeon, but sustained and soothed
> By an unfaltering trust, approach thy grave
> Like one that wraps the drapery of his couch
> About him, and lies down to pleasant dreams.'

On July 1, 1986, the weary body of Edward Curtis Wells entered that silent hall of death. But to all who knew and honored him, it seemed his gallant soul had taken flight on silvered wings.

Appendix: Selected List of Honors and Awards

Lawrence Sperry Award, 1942, for the B-17: "...outstanding contributions to the art of airplane design with special reference to four-engined aircraft"

Young Man of the Year, Seattle Junior Chamber of Commerce, 1943

Fawcett Aviation Award, 1944, for the B-29: "The greatest single contribution for the advancement of scientific aviation during the year"

Honorary Doctorate, Portland University, 1946

President's Certificate of Merit, 1948: "...meritorious service in aiding the United States during the prosecution of the recent war"

Honorary Doctor of Science degree, Willamette University, 1953

Elected President of the Institute of Aeronautical Sciences, 1958

Elected Honorary Fellow of the American Institute of Aeronautics and Astronautics, 1973

Elected Prestigious Honorary Fellow, American Institute of Aeronautics and Astronautics, 1974: "...for his outstanding fundamental contributions to aeronautics throughout a dedicated career beginning with the B-17 'Flying Fortress' and culminating [in] the B-47 'Jumbo Jet'"

National Aeronautic Association, Elder Statesman of Aviation, 1978

Daniel Guggenheim Medal, 1980: "...outstanding contributions in the design and production of some of the world's most famous commercial and military aircraft"

Elected Fellow of the Society of Automotive Engineers, 1980: "...for exceptional contributions to the advancement of automotive technology"

Pathfinder Award, Museum of Flight, 1983

Elected Fellow, American Association for the Advancement of Science, 1984

Tony Jannus Award, 1985: "...outstanding contributions to the development of complex aerospace systems and significant accomplishments in the design and production of a long line of the world's most famous military and commercial aircraft"

Inducted posthumously into the National Hall of Aviation Fame, 1991

Note on Sources

As I explained in the Preface, the main sources for this book came from Ed Wells's own files: letters, photos, memoranda, patents, magazine articles, copies of speeches. I was also aided by correspondence from and conversations with Walter J. Boyne, Keith Ferris, Charles Geer, Richard Geer, Marge Blair Hovey, William Jury, John Kane, Margaret Wells Ketteringham, Curtis E. LeMay, George Martin, Jean-Claude Peter, Jim Rostirolla, Donald Sachs, George Schairer, Jay Spenser, Paul Spitzer, Laurie Wells Tull, Dale Turner, Dorothy Wells, Edward Elliott Wells, and T. Wilson. Donald A. Schmechel's 1985 taped interview with Ed Wells was another source, as was Lloyd Goodmanson's 1979 videotape on the development of the B-52.

The following publications were helpful: *The Boeing Log Book* (Seattle: Boeing Archives, 1991); Peter M. Bowers, *Boeing Aircraft since 1916* (1968; reprint Annapolis: Naval Institute Press, 1989); Walter Boyne, *Boeing B-52: A Documentary History* (New York: Jane's, 1982); Martin Caidin, *Flying Forts* (New York: Hawthorn, 1968); Thomas Collison, *Flying Fortress* (New York: Scribner's, 1943); Collison *The Superfortress Is Born* (New York: Duell, Sloan and Pearce, 1945); William H. Cook, "The First Boeing High-Speed Wind Tunnel" (pamphlet), Boeing Archives, 1990; "Flight Path" (pamphlet), Boeing Archives, 1990; Harold Mansfield, *Vision: A Saga of the Sky* (New York: Duell, Sloan and Pearce, 1956); *Year by Year, 75 Years of Boeing History* (Seattle: Boeing Archives, 1991).

Index

Boldface numbers refer to illustrations